Cook's Corner

# Perfect
# Pasta

igloobooks

Published in 2018
by Igloo Books Ltd
Cottage Farm
Sywell
NN6 0BJ
www.igloobooks.com

Food photography and recipe development
© StockFood, The Food Media Agency
Additional imagery: © iStock / Getty Images
Cover images: © iStock / Getty Images

STA002 0218
2 4 6 8 10 9 7 5 3 1
ISBN 978-1-78810-177-6

Designed by Nicholas Gage
Interiors designed by Simon Parker
Edited by Jasmin Peppiatt

Printed and manufactured in China

Cook's Corner

Perfect
Pasta

# Contents

## Cook's Corner

### Perfect Pasta
# Meat dishes

# Chicken pasta salad with cheese crouton

SERVES: 4 | PREP TIME: 15 MINUTES | COOKING TIME: 30 MINUTES

## INGREDIENTS

2 chicken breasts, skin on

1 red pepper, deseeded and chopped

2 tbsp olive oil

300 g / 10 oz / 1 ½ cups fusilli pasta

1 handful black olives

4 slices of baguette, 1 cm (½ in) thick

60 g / 2 oz / ½ cup goat's cheese log, sliced

mixed salad, to serve

## METHOD

1. Preheat the oven to 200°C / 400F / gas 6. Place the chicken and pepper in a roasting tin. Drizzle with 1 tablespoon of oil. Roast for 25 minutes.

2. Leave the chicken to cool in the pan then tear into shreds. Place in a bowl with the pepper and olives.

3. Cook the pasta according to the packet instructions. Drain then tip into the bowl with the chicken. Drizzle with the remaining olive oil.

4. Toast the baguettes brushed with a little oil under a hot grill until golden. Top with the goat's cheese and grill again until the cheese is bubbling.

5. Serve with the chicken pasta salad and some mixed leaves on the side.

# Lasagne

SERVES: 4-6 | PREP TIME: 30 MINUTES | COOKING TIME: 3 HOURS 10 MINUTES

## INGREDIENTS

10 lasagne sheets
2 tbsp Parmesan, grated

FOR THE TOMATO SAUCE:
1 tbsp olive oil
1 onion, peeled and finely chopped
2 carrots, peeled and thickly sliced
2 courgettes (zucchini), thickly sliced
500 g / 1 lb / 2 ¼ cups minced beef
120 ml / 4 fl. oz / ½ cup white wine
800 g / 1 ¾ lbs oz / 4 cups tomatoes
550 ml / 1 pint / 2 cups beef stock

FOR THE BÉCHAMEL SAUCE:
2 tbsp butter
2 tbsp plain (all-purpose) flour
700 ml / 1 ¼ pints / 2 ¾ cups milk
nutmeg, grated

## METHOD

1. For the tomato sauce, fry the onion, carrots and courgette in oil for 10 minutes. Add the beef, break it up, then add the tomatoes and wine. Leave to simmer for 2 hours. Add more stock as it absorbs.

2. For the béchamel sauce, heat the butter in a pan, then stir in the flour to make a roux. Whisk in the milk a little at a time. Simmer for 10 minutes. Whisk until thick. Add the nutmeg.

3. Preheat the oven to 190°C (170° fan) / 375F / gas 5. Add a third of the tomato sauce in the bottom of a baking dish, then a quarter of the béchamel, then add two lasagne sheets next to each other.

4. Repeat the process until all the lasagne sheets and sauces are used up. Cover the top layer of lasagne with béchamel and sprinkle over the Parmesan.

5. Bake in the oven for 40 minutes until the pasta is tender. Leave to rest for 10 minutes before serving.

# Tagliatelle carbonara

SERVES: 4 | PREP TIME: 5 MINUTES | COOKING TIME: 12 MINUTES

## INGREDIENTS

500 g / 1 lb 2 oz / 2 cups tagliatelle

2 tbsp butter

12 slices pancetta, chopped

4 egg yolks

100 ml / 3 ½ fl. oz / ½ cup double (heavy) cream

2 tbsp Parmesan, grated

## METHOD

1. Cook the pasta in boiling salted water according to the packet instructions.

2. Heat the butter in a pan and fry the pancetta until cooked through and golden.

3. Whisk the egg yolks and Parmesan into the cream.

4. Drain the pasta, return to the pan and, working quickly, scrape the pancetta and butter into the pan and toss.

5. Toss off the heat with the egg and cream mixture then serve immediately.

# Fusilli with bacon

SERVES: 4 | PREP TIME: 5 MINUTES | COOKING TIME: 15 MINUTES

## INGREDIENTS

500g / 1 lb / 2 cups fusilli pasta

60g / 2 oz / ¼ cup butter

80 g / 3 oz / ⅓ cup diced pancetta or smoked bacon

½ bunch tarragon leaves, chopped

salt and pepper

## METHOD

1. Cook the pasta in boiling salted water for 10 minutes or according to packet instructions.

2. Drain, reserving a little of the cooking water.

3. Meanwhile cook the pancetta in the butter until golden and cooked through.

4. Throw in the tarragon leaves and 2 tablespoons of cooking water, then toss with the pasta.

5. Season with salt and pepper then serve.

11

# Chicken lasagne

SERVES: 4 | PREP TIME: 30 MINUTES | COOKING TIME: 1 HOUR 40 MINS

## INGREDIENTS

150 ml / 5 fl. oz / ⅔ cup beef stock

12 lasagne sheets, pre-cooked

2 tbsp Parmesan, grated

### FOR THE SAUCE:

1 tbsp butter

1 tbsp olive oil

1 onion, peeled and finely chopped

2 celery stalks, finely chopped

2 cloves garlic, finely chopped

2 carrots, finely chopped

120 g / 4 oz / ½ cup pancetta, cubed

500 g / 1 lb chicken breast, chopped

120 ml / 4 fl. oz / ½ cup white wine

800 g / 1 ¾ lbs / 4 cups tomatoes

### FOR THE BÉCHAMEL SAUCE:

2 tbsp butter

2 tbsp plain (all-purpose) flour

700 ml / 1 ¼ pints / 2 ¾ cups milk

1 bay leaf

nutmeg, grated

## METHOD

1. To make the tomato sauce, heat the butter with a little oil in a pan and add the finely chopped vegetables and pancetta and cook for about 10 minutes.

2. Add the chicken and cook until golden. Season with salt and pepper. Add the wine and tomatoes and simmer for about 45 minutes.

3. Make the béchamel by heating the butter in a pan until foaming, then stirring in the flour to make a paste.

4. Whisk in the milk a little at a time. Add the bay leaf and simmer for 10 minutes, whisking frequently until thick. Season and add a little freshly grated nutmeg.

5. Preheat the oven to 190°C (170° fan) / 375F / gas 5.

6. Lay 4 lasagne sheets followed by a third of the bolognese sauce in the bottom of a baking dish, then a quarter of the béchamel. Repeat twice more, then cover the top layer with béchamel and sprinkle over the Parmesan.

7. Bake in the oven for 40 minutes.

8. Leave to rest for 10 minutes before serving.

# Lasagne with mushrooms

SERVES: 4 | PREP TIME: 30 MINUTES | COOKING TIME: 2 HOURS 40 MINS

## INGREDIENTS

150 ml / 5 fl. oz / ⅔ cup beef stock

12 lasagne sheets

2 tbsp Parmesan, grated

### FOR THE FILLING:

1 tbsp butter

2 tbsp olive oil

1 onion, peeled and finely chopped

2 celery stalks, finely chopped

2 cloves garlic, finely chopped

2 carrots, finely chopped

200 g / 6 ½ oz / ¾ cup mushrooms

120 g / 4 oz / ½ cup pancetta, cubed

500 g / 1 lb / 2 cups minced beef

120 ml / 4 fl. oz / ½ cup white wine

800 g / 1 ¾ lbs / 4 cups tomatoes

450 ml / 1 pint / 2 cups beef stock

### FOR THE BÉCHAMEL SAUCE:

2 tbsp butter

2 tbsp plain (all-purpose) flour

700 ml / 1 ¼ pints / 2 ¾ cups milk

1 bay leaf

nutmeg, grated

## METHOD

1. Heat the butter with a little oil in a pan and add the finely chopped vegetables, the mushrooms and pancetta and cook for about 10 minutes.

2. Add the beef, wine, tomatoes and half the stock, then lower the heat. Partially cover the pan and leave to simmer for 2 hours, adding more stock as it absorbs.

3. To make the béchamel, heat the butter in a pan then stir in the flour to make a paste. Whisk in the milk a little at a time. Add the bay leaf and simmer for 10 minutes, whisking until thick. Season and add freshly grated nutmeg.

4. Preheat the oven to 190°C (170° fan) / 375F / gas 5. Add 4 lasagne sheets then a third of the filling in the bottom of a baking dish, then a quarter of the béchamel.

5. Repeat twice more, then cover the top with béchamel and sprinkle over the Parmesan. Bake in the oven for 40 minutes. Leave to rest for 10 minutes before serving.

# Ham cannelloni

SERVES: 4 | PREP TIME: 25 MINUTES | COOKING TIME: 15 MINUTES

## INGREDIENTS

FOR THE FILLING:

130 g / 4 ½ oz / ½ cup ham, chopped

400 g / 13 ½ oz / 1 ½ cups ricotta

2 tbsp Parmesan, grated

salt and pepper

12 cannelloni tubes or 12 sheets lasagne

FOR THE TOMATO SAUCE:

2 tbsp olive oil

1 clove of garlic, chopped

800 g / 1 lb 12 oz canned chopped tomatoes

½ bunch basil, chopped

2 mozzarella balls, sliced

## METHOD

1. Preheat the oven to 180°C (160° fan) / 350F / gas 4. Mix the ham, ricotta, Parmesan and seasoning together in a bowl.

2. Spoon into the tubes or onto the lasagne sheets and roll up the sheets to make 12 cylinders, then lay in a greased baking dish.

3. Heat the oil in a pan and add the garlic and tomatoes. Leave to simmer, topped up with half a can of water, for 10 minutes. Add the basil and season. Spoon over the cannelloni.

4. Lay the slices of mozzarella over the top and drizzle with olive oil then bake for 15 minutes until bubbling.

# Parma ham pasta parcels

SERVES: 4 | PREP TIME: 5 MINUTES | COOKING TIME: 35 MINUTES

## INGREDIENTS

200 g / 7 oz / 2 cups penne pasta

8 slices Parma ham

1 tbsp olive oil

FOR THE SAUCE:

1 onion, peeled

2 cloves garlic, peeled

400g / 14 oz / 2 cups chopped tomatoes

2 tbsp basil

## METHOD

1. Cook the pasta in boiling salted water according to the packet instructions. Drain, toss with a little olive oil and keep warm.

2. Mix the sauce ingredients in a blender, according to the manufacturer's instructions, until smooth.

3. Add 1 tablespoon of olive oil to a pan and add the sauce. Cook gently for 20 minutes until the onion taste has gone and the sauce has reduced.

4. Toss the pasta in the sauce.

5. Lay 2 slices of ham on each plate in a cross and spoon the pasta into the middle.

6. Fold the ends of the ham over the pasta to form a parcel. Spoon a little extra sauce around to serve.

# Tagliatelle with grilled chicken

SERVES: 4 | PREP TIME: 10 MINUTES | COOKING TIME: 15 MINUTES

## INGREDIENTS

2 chicken breasts

1 yellow or orange pepper,
deseeded and sliced into pieces

1 tbsp olive oil

500 g / 1 lb 2 oz / 2 cups fresh tagliatelle

6 cherry tomatoes, sliced into halves

a small handful of basil leaves, to serve

freshly ground black pepper, to serve

## METHOD

1. Cut the chicken into small pieces and toss it with the sliced pepper and oil and season.

2. Heat a griddle pan until smoking and griddle the chicken and pepper until cooked through.

3. Meanwhile, cook the pasta in boiling water according to the packet instructions. Drain and toss with a little oil and keep warm.

4. Once the chicken and pepper is cooked, mix it with the pasta and cherry tomato halves.

5. Divide between four bowls and top with a few basil leaves and a grind of black pepper.

6. Serve immediately.

# Spaghetti with turkey

SERVES: 4 | PREP TIME: 20 MINUTES | COOKING TIME: 20 MINUTES

## INGREDIENTS

8 turkey escalopes

4 tbsp olive oil

1 courgette (zucchini), cut into batons

1 clove garlic, lightly crushed

4 sprigs thyme

400g / 13 ½ oz / 1 ½ cups spaghetti

4 tbsp pesto

## METHOD

1. Place the escalopes between 2 sheets of clingfilm and bat out until quite thin.

2. Heat the olive oil divided between two pans. Sear the escalopes for 2 minutes on each side.

3. Remove from the pan and drain on kitchen paper. Add the courgette batons with the garlic and thyme. Sauté until tender and golden.

4. Drain on kitchen paper.

5. Lay out the turkey escalopes and lay a few slices of courgette on each one. Roll up and secure with a toothpick.

6. Cook the pasta in boiling salted water according to the packet instructions.

7. Drain not too thoroughly and toss with the pesto.

8. Return the escalopes to the pan. Cover with a lid and cook for another 3 minutes until the turkey is cooked through. Serve with the spaghetti.

# Orecchiette with apples, spinach and Parma ham

SERVES: 4 | PREP TIME: 10 MINUTES | COOKING TIME: 14 MINUTES

## INGREDIENTS

500 g / 1 lb / 2 cups orecchiette pasta

2 tbsp butter

1 eating apple, peeled, quartered, cored and sliced

8 slices Parma ham, chopped

2 handfuls baby spinach leaves

2 tbsp pecorino, grated

## METHOD

1. Cook the pasta in boiling salted water according to the packet instructions.

2. Meanwhile heat the butter and cook the apple until just tender but holding its shape.

3. Add the Parma ham and remove from the heat.

4. Drain the pasta, reserving some of the cooking water.

5. Toss the pasta with the apples and ham, adding a tablespoon of cooking water to lubricate. Season with salt and pepper.

6. Toss through the spinach leaves, add the pecorino and serve.

# Fusilli with marinated lamb

SERVES: 4 | PREP TIME: 15 MINUTES | COOKING TIME: 30 MINUTES

## INGREDIENTS

300 g / 10 oz lamb fillet

2 tbsp raisins or sultanas

100 ml / 3 ½ fl oz / ½ cup Marsala

salt and pepper

500 g / 1 lb 2 oz / 2 cups fusilli pasta

1 tbsp butter

½ bunch basil

Parmesan, grated, to serve

## METHOD

1. Slice the lamb into strips and marinate with the sultanas and Marsala for 15 minutes.

2. Cook the pasta in boiling water according to the packet instructions. Drain and keep warm.

3. Heat a frying pan until very hot, remove the lamb from marinade and pat dry, then fry briskly until still pink in the middle but coloured and cooked on the outside.

4. Add the marinade and sultanas to the pan and deglaze, reducing the liquid until syrupy.

5. Stir in the butter so the sauce is shiny.

6. Toss the pasta with the sauce and the lamb. Stir in the basil and serve with Parmesan.

# Macaroni with beef

SERVES: 6 | PREP TIME: 15 MINUTES | COOKING TIME: 30 MINUTES

## INGREDIENTS

600 g / 1 lb 5 oz / 4 cups stewing beef, cubed

1 onion, peeled and chopped

1 clove garlic, peeled and chopped

50 ml beef stock

2 tbsp barbecue sauce

1 tbsp tomato puree

500 g / 1 lb 2 oz / 4 ½ cups macaroni pasta

## METHOD

1. Pat the beef dry to remove any excess liquid, season, then fry in a large pan for around 3-5 minutes to seal all sides.

2. Remove the meat from the pan and keep warm on a plate covered in foil. Place the chopped onion, garlic, stock, barbecue sauce and tomato puree in the pan. Stir well until the onion is fried and the stock has mostly evaporated.

3. Meanwhile, cook the pasta according to the packet instructions. Drain and toss with a little butter, if required, to prevent sticking.

4. Once the pasta is cooked, divide it between six warm plates and arrange the cooked beef, onions and barbecue sauce on top.

# Ravioli with duck liver and mushrooms

SERVES: 4-6 | PREP TIME: 1 HOUR | COOKING TIME: 10-12 MINUTES |

CHILLING TIME: 30 MINUTES

## INGREDIENTS

### FOR THE PASTA:

500 g / 1 lb 2 oz / 2 cups '00' flour
(Italian super-white flour)

6 eggs

### FOR THE FILLING:

3 tbsp butter

200 g / 7 oz / ¾ cup wild mushrooms,
finely chopped

150 g / 5 oz / ⅔ cup flat mushrooms,
finely chopped

½ onion, peeled and finely chopped

2 tbsp Parmesan, grated

1 tbsp flat-leaved parsley, finely chopped

### TO SERVE:

100 g / 3 ½ oz / ½ cup mushrooms, sliced

butter

4 thick slices duck liver pâté

Parmesan, grated

## METHOD

1. Combine the pasta ingredients and knead
   for 5 minutes. Cover with film and chill
   for 30 minutes.

2. For the filling, heat the butter in a pan and
   fry the finely chopped wild mushrooms, flat
   mushrooms and onion. Stir in the Parmesan
   and parsley then season.

3. Using a pasta machine, roll out the dough
   as thinly as possible and 10 cm (4 in) wide.

4. Place 1 teaspoon of the filling from step 2
   in the middle of the sheet at one end. Repeat
   all the way along at 5 cm (2 in) intervals, then
   brush a little water around each filling in a
   circle. Place another sheet of pasta on top
   then cut out the ravioli shapes.

5. Heat 2 tablespoons of butter in a pan and
   cook the sliced mushrooms specified in the
   'to serve' ingredients list.

6. In another pan, lightly salt the pâté slices
   and sear on each side for 30 seconds,
   then cook for 1 minute more.

7. Bring a pan of water to the boil and cook the
   ravioli for 4 minutes. Remove carefully then
   toss with butter and Parmesan.

8. Serve with the warm mushrooms scattered
   over and a slice of pâté on top.

# Tagliatelle with beef and cherry tomatoes

SERVES: 4 | PREP TIME: 5 MINUTES | COOKING TIME: 20 MINUTES

## INGREDIENTS

300 g / 10 oz / 1 ¼ cups cherry tomatoes

2 beef steaks, sliced into strips

1 onion, chopped

1 tbsp olive oil

500 g / 1 lb / 2 cups tagliatelle

1 tbsp basil, chopped

freshly ground black pepper, to serve

## METHOD

1. Preheat the oven to 200°C / 400F / gas 6.

2. Place the cherry tomatoes, beef strips and chopped onions in a roasting tin and drizzle with oil. Season well and roast in the oven for at least 20 minutes or until well cooked.

3. Meanwhile cook the pasta in boiling salted water according to the packet instructions.

4. Drain the pasta.

5. Toss the pasta with the tomatoes and their roasting juices, the beef and the chopped basil.

6. Adjust the seasoning and serve with a good grind of black pepper.

# Pappardelle with ham

SERVES: 4 | PREP TIME: 15 MINUTES | COOKING TIME: 10 MINUTES

## INGREDIENTS

400 g / 14 oz / 3 ½ cups pappardelle pasta

6 slices of cured ham, such as Parma

2 bunches rocket

60 g butter

110 g / 4 oz / 1 cup Parmesan, grated

250 ml / 9 fl. oz / 1 cup crème fraiche

salt and pepper

## METHOD

1. Cook the pasta in a large pan of boiling salted water until al dente or just tender.

2. Drain and toss with a little olive oil to prevent sticking.

3. Cut the cured ham in half lengthways.

4. Roughly chop the rocket.

5. Heat the butter in a pan, add the pasta and stir. Sprinkle over the Parmesan then add the crème fraiche. Season and mix well.

6. Divide the pasta between four bowls then lay the ham and rocket on top before serving.

# Fusilli with artichokes

SERVES: 4 | PREP TIME: 5 MINUTES | COOKING TIME: 12 MINUTES

## INGREDIENTS

500 g / 1 lb / 2 cups fusilli pasta

2 tbsp olive oil

1 clove garlic, finely chopped

1 tbsp thyme leaves

300 ml / 10 fl. oz / 1 ¼ cups passata

285 g / 10 oz / 1 jar artichoke hearts, halved

1 rasher of bacon, cooked

2 tbsp Parmesan, finely grated

## METHOD

1. Cook the pasta in boiling salted water according to the packet instructions.

2. Meanwhile heat the oil in a pan and gently fry the garlic with the thyme.

3. Add the passata and a splash of pasta cooking water and leave to simmer for 10 minutes.

4. Chop up the rasher of bacon and add this, along with the artichokes, to the passata.

5. Drain the pasta and toss with the sauce.

6. Serve scattered with Parmesan.

# Pasta with artichokes and Serrano ham

SERVES: 4 | PREP TIME: 5 MINUTES | COOKING TIME: 15 MINUTES

## INGREDIENTS

500 g / 1 lb / 2 cups dried fusilli pasta

2 tbsp olive oil

1 clove garlic, chopped

285 g / 10 oz artichoke hearts, drained

4 slices Serrano ham

## METHOD

1. Cook the pasta in boiling salted water according to the packet instructions. Save a small mug of the cooking water.

2. Meanwhile, heat the olive oil in a pan and gently fry the garlic.

3. Add the artichokes and ham and warm through.

4. Drain the pasta then toss in the pan with a little of the cooking water to amalgamate.

5. Serve sprinkled with Parmesan cheese.

# Pasta, cheese and ham frittata

SERVES: 4 | PREP TIME: 10 MINUTES | COOKING TIME: 20 MINUTES

## INGREDIENTS

300 g / 10 oz / 1 ¼ cups macaroni

4 thick slices ham, chopped

4 tbsp Parmesan or Gruyère, grated

3 sprigs thyme, leaves only

5 eggs, beaten

## METHOD

1. Preheat the oven to 180°C / 350F / gas 5.

2. Cook the pasta in boiling, salted water according to the packet instructions.

3. Meanwhile whisk together the eggs, ham, cheese and thyme and season with salt and pepper.

4. Drain the pasta then stir into the eggs.

5. Pour into a large ovenproof frying pan and cook for about 20 minutes until the eggs are cooked through.

6. Serve warm or cold.

# Farfalle with chicken and vegetables

SERVES: 4 | PREP TIME: 10 MINUTES | COOKING TIME: 25 MINUTES

## INGREDIENTS

500 g / 1 lb / 2 cups farfalle
2 tbsp olive oil
1 onion, peeled and sliced
2 chicken breasts, chopped
140 g / 5 oz / ½ jar artichoke hearts
2 red peppers, 'cheeks' cut off
1 sprig oregano

## METHOD

1. Cook the pasta in boiling salted water according to the packet instructions. Drain, reserving a little of the water.

2. Heat the oil in a pan and cook the onion for about 15 minutes until soft and sweet.

3. Add the chicken and peppers and cook briskly until golden.

4. Add the artichokes and oregano and season with salt and pepper.

5. Toss the pasta with the chicken, adding a little cooking water to lubricate.

# Spirali pasta with Parma ham and basil

SERVES: 4 | PREP TIME: 5 MINUTES | COOKING TIME: 15 MINUTES

## INGREDIENTS

500 g / 1 lb 2 oz / 2 cups spirali pasta

3 tbsp butter

4 slices Parma ham, cut into fine strips

4 tbsp Parmesan

1 tbsp basil, chopped

## METHOD

1. Cook the pasta in boiling salted water according to the packet instructions. Drain, reserving a little of the cooking water and toss with a little oil.

2. Heat the butter in a pan and add the Parma ham.

3. Toss in the pasta and 2 tablespoons of water, then stir in the Parmesan and basil.

4. Season with salt and pepper and serve.

# Linguine with duck liver pâté and mushrooms

SERVES: 4 | PREP TIME: 10 MINUTES | COOKING TIME: 15 MINUTES

## INGREDIENTS

500 g / 1 lb 2 oz / 2 cups linguine

4 thick slices duck liver pâté

100 g / 3 ½ oz / ½ cup mushrooms, thickly sliced

2 tbsp butter

Parmesan, grated

## METHOD

1. Cook the linguine in boiling salted water according to the packet instructions.

2. Drain and toss with a little butter.

3. Heat the butter in a pan and cook the mushrooms. Season and keep warm.

4. Heat a frying pan, lightly salt the liver pâté slices and sear on each side for 30 seconds. Cook for 1 minute more. Remove from the pan.

5. Serve the linguine tossed with the mushrooms and their butter and Parmesan.

6. Top with a slice of pâté.

# Conchiglie with asparagus and beef

SERVES: 4 | PREP TIME: 10 MINUTES | COOKING TIME: 12 MINUTES

●●●●●●●●●●●●●●●●●●●●●●●●●●●●

## INGREDIENTS

500 g / 1 lb / 2 cups conchiglie pasta

8 stalks asparagus, woody ends snapped off and cut into short lengths

60 g / 2 oz / ¼ cup butter

1 clove garlic, sliced

¼ lemon, grated zest

8 slices air-dried beef, sliced into strips

## METHOD

1. Cook the pasta in boiling salted water according to the packet instructions.

2. Add the asparagus 3 minutes before the end of the cooking time.

3. Meanwhile heat the butter and garlic in a pan, then add the beef and zest and toss together.

4. Drain the pasta, reserving a little of the water and toss with the butter sauce, adding 1-2 tablespoons of reserved cooking water to amalgamate the sauce.

# Tagliatelle with duck liver pâté

SERVES: 4 | PREP TIME: 5 MINUTES | COOKING TIME: 20 MINUTES

## INGREDIENTS

4 thick slices duck liver pâté

250 g / 9 oz / 1 cup wild mushrooms

400 ml / 14 fl. oz / 1 ½ cups veal demi-glace
(reduced veal stock)

salt and pepper

500 g / 1 lb 2 oz / 2 cups fresh tagliatelle

1 tbsp butter

## METHOD

1. Heat a frying pan until very hot and sear the duck
liver pâté for 30 seconds on each side then leave to
cook for 1 minute.

2. Remove to a plate and keep warm.

3. Add the mushrooms to the pan and fry briskly
until the liquid evaporates. Pour in the demi-glace
and reduce by a third. Season well and keep hot.

4. Cook the tagliatelle in boiling salted water
according to the packet instructions.

5. Drain and toss with the butter.

6. Serve with the duck liver pâté and mushrooms
on top and the sauce spooned over.

# Cannelloni wrapped in ham

SERVES: 4 | PREP TIME: 20 MINUTES | COOKING TIME: 10 MINUTES

## INGREDIENTS

3 tomatoes

500g / 1 lb / 2 cups ricotta

½ bunch basil, chopped

1 bunch chives, finely chopped

salt and pepper

12 cannelloni tubes

12 slices ham

olive oil

## METHOD

1. Plunge the tomatoes into boiling water and leave for 30 seconds. Remove and peel away the skin. Deseed and dice the flesh.

2. Mix the tomato concasse in a bowl with 1 tablespoon of olive oil, salt and pepper. Stir in the basil, chives and ricotta. Taste and adjust the seasoning, if desired.

3. Cook the cannelloni tubes in boiling salted water for 10 minutes. Drain and pat dry.

4. Working quickly, use a teaspoon or piping bag to stuff the tubes with equal amounts of filling.

5. Wrap the tubes in a slice of ham and serve.

# Linguine bolognese

SERVES: 4 | PREP TIME: 15 MINUTES | COOKING TIME: 30 MINUTES

## INGREDIENTS

500 g / 1 lb / 2 cups linguine

3 tbsp olive oil

2 onions, peeled and finely chopped

2 cloves garlic, peeled and finely chopped

1 pack pancetta or bacon lardons

500 g / 1 lb / 2 cups minced beef

800 g / 1 ¾ lbs / 4 cups chopped tomatoes

2 tbsp parsley, chopped

100 g / 3 ½ oz / ½ cup Parmesan, grated

## METHOD

1. Heat the oil in a pan and sweat the onion and garlic until soft. Add the pancetta and fry until the fat runs.

2. Add the mince and break it up with a wooden spoon, stirring frequently until cooked.

3. Season with salt and pepper, then add the tomatoes.

4. Partially cover and simmer for 15 minutes.

5. Meanwhile, cook the pasta in boiling salted water according to the packet instructions.

6. Drain and toss with a little oil.

7. Stir the parsley through the sauce.

8. Divide the pasta between four plates then place the bolognese sauce on top.

9. Serve with grated Parmesan.

# Beef in cream sauce

SERVES: 2 | PREP TIME: 20 MINUTES | COOKING TIME: 20 MINUTES

## INGREDIENTS

120 g / 4 ¼ oz dried spaghetti

2 tbsp olive oil

2 x 225 g / 8 oz fillet steak

1 shallot, diced

1 clove of garlic, minced

150 ml / 5 ¼ fl. oz / ⅔ cup beef stock

100 ml / 3 ½ fl. oz / ½ cup double (heavy) cream

25 g / 1 oz Parmesan cheese, grated

## METHOD

1. Bring a pan of water to the boil. Cook the pasta according to the packet instructions. Once cooked, drain and set aside.

2. While the pasta is cooking, pour the oil over the steaks and season. Place a frying pan onto a high heat. Once smoking, add the steaks.

3. Cook for 8 minutes on each side, as desired. Remove and cover with foil to rest.

4. Turn the heat down to medium. Add the shallot and garlic. Cook for 2 minutes then add the beef stock and cream. Let the sauce boil and thicken.

5. Slice the steaks. Put in the sauce to heat through.

6. Toss the cheese through the pasta with a drizzle of olive oil. Add to serving bowls and top with the sliced steak and cream sauce.

# Spaghetti with sausage

SERVES: 2 | PREP TIME: 10 MINUTES | COOKING TIME: 25 MINUTES

## INGREDIENTS

2 tbsp olive oil

4 Italian or Sicilian style sausages

1 onion, diced

1 clove of garlic, minced

1 tsp dried oregano

400 g / 14 oz canned chopped tomatoes

120 g / 4 ¼ oz spaghetti

sea salt and cracked black pepper

fresh basil, to garnish

## METHOD

1.  Heat the oil in a pan over a medium heat. Add the sausages and cook for 8 minutes until browned. Remove then cut them into slices.

2.  Add the onion to the pan and cook for 4-5 minutes. Add the garlic and oregano and cook for a further minute. Return the sausage to the pan and add the tomatoes. Cover and leave to cook for 12-15 minutes.

3.  In a pan of boiling water, cook the pasta according to the packet instructions. Add a little pasta water to the tomato sauce if it has become thick. If not, drain the pasta and add the spaghetti to the sausage and tomato.

4.  Season the pasta before adding to serving plates and garnishing with basil.

41

# Penne chicken pasta bake

SERVES: 4-6  |  PREP TIME: 10 MINUTES  |  COOKING TIME: 45 MINUTES

## INGREDIENTS

500 g / 1 lb 1 oz penne pasta

2 tbsp olive oil

1 large onion, diced

2 cloves of garlic, finely chopped

400 g / 14 oz chicken breasts, cubed

1 tsp dried oregano

1 tbsp tomato puree

400 g / 14 oz canned chopped tomatoes

100 g / 3 ½ oz / ⅔ cup black olives, pitted

a small bunch of fresh basil, chopped

150 g / 5 ¼ oz / 1 ½ cups mozzarella cheese, grated

sea salt and cracked black pepper

## METHOD

1. Add the pasta to a large pan of boiling water. Cook for 15 minutes, drain then set aside.

2. Heat the oil in a large pan over a medium heat. Add the onion and fry for 4-5 minutes until soft. Add the garlic and cook for a further minute before adding the chicken. Fry for around 5 minutes until browned, add the oregano and tomato puree followed by the chopped tomatoes, olives and most of the basil. Season and cover and cook for 10 minutes.

3. Preheat the oven to 180°C (160°C fan) / 350F / gas 4.

4. Add the pasta and tomato sauce to an ovenproof dish and mix to combine. Cover with the grated cheese and bake in the oven for around 25 minutes until the cheese is melted and starting to colour.

5. Top with the reserved basil leaves and serve.

# Spaghetti with bacon and asparagus

SERVES: 1 | PREP TIME: 5 MINUTES | COOKING TIME: 20 MINUTES

## INGREDIENTS

100 g / 3 ½ oz spaghetti

2 tbsp olive oil

75 g / 2 ½ oz bacon lardons

75 g / 2 ½ oz asparagus tips

50 g / 1 ¾ oz cherry tomatoes

25 g Parmesan cheese, grated

parsley, to garnish

## METHOD

1. Cook the pasta in a pan of boiling water as per the packet instructions.

2. At the same time, heat half the oil in a frying pan over a medium heat. Add the bacon and fry for 8-10 minutes until starting to crisp at the edges.

3. Add the asparagus and cherry tomatoes to the pan. Cook for a further 5 minutes until softened.

4. Add the pasta to the pan with the bacon and vegetables and toss to combine, adding the remaining oil to coat the pasta.

5. Place on a serving plate and sprinkle over the cheese and garnish with the herbs.

# Chicken meatballs

SERVES: 2 | PREP TIME: 15 MINUTES | COOKING TIME: 15 MINUTES

## INGREDIENTS

300 g / 10 ½ oz chicken mince

a small bunch of basil, chopped

a small bunch of parsley, chopped

1 tbsp dried oregano, chopped

1 egg, beaten

1 clove of garlic, minced

500 ml / 17 fl. oz / 2 cups chicken stock

250 g / 9 oz passata

150 g / 5 ¼ oz spaghetti

50 g / 1 ¾ oz Parmesan cheese, grated

## METHOD

1. Combine the chicken, herbs, egg and garlic in a mixing bowl. Season before mixing and forming into balls using your hands.

2. Heat the stock in a sauté pan with high sides until near boiling. Poach the meatballs in the stock for 12-15 minutes until cooked through.

3. Heat the passata in a pan until warmed through.

4. Cook the pasta in a pan of boiling salted water as per the packet instructions. Drain when cooked.

5. To serve, divide the pasta between two plates and top with the tomato sauce and then the meatballs.

6. Sprinkle with the grated cheese.

# Spaghetti with tomato and aubergine

SERVES: 2 | PREP TIME: 10 MINUTES | COOKING TIME: 20 MINUTES

## INGREDIENTS

120 g / 4 ¼ oz spaghetti

2 tbsp olive oil

1 shallot, diced

1 clove of garlic, minced

1 aubergine (eggplant), diced

chicken breast, cooked and cubed

100 g / 3 ½ oz cherry tomatoes, halved

1 lemon, juice and zest

a pinch of chilli (chili) flakes

a handful of chopped parsley

25 g / 1 oz Parmesan cheese, grated

## METHOD

1.  Cook the pasta in a large pan of water as per the packet instructions. Drain, reserving some of the water, then set aside.

2.  Heat the oil in a pan over a medium heat. Add the shallot and garlic. Cook for 1-2 minutes. Add the aubergine, chicken and tomatoes to the pan and continue to fry for 10 minutes until the tomatoes have broken down and aubergine is starting to colour.

3.  Add the lemon and chilli flakes to the pan with a splash of the pasta water. Add the cooked spaghetti to the pan and toss to coat and warm through.

4.  Add the chopped parsley to the pan. Place the spaghetti on serving plates. Top with Parmesan.

# Lasagne soup

SERVES: 4-6 | PREP TIME: 15 MINUTES | COOKING TIME: 30 MINUTES

## INGREDIENTS

1 tbsp olive oil

1 large onion, diced

2 carrots, diced

2 celery sticks, diced

2 cloves of garlic, minced

2 tsp dried oregano

1 tsp dried basil

500 g / 1 lb 1 oz beef mince

400 g / 14 oz canned chopped tomatoes

a handful of fresh basil, chopped

250 g / 8 ¾ oz farfalle

200 g / 7 oz / 2 cups mozzarella cheese, grated

## METHOD

1. Heat the oil in a large casserole pan over a medium heat. Add the onion, carrot and celery and cook for 6-8 minutes. Add the garlic and cook for a further minute until fragrant.

2. Add the herbs and beef mince. Brown the meat for 3 minutes before adding the tomatoes and seasoning. Turn up the heat until boiling, turn back down to a simmer. Cover and cook for 20 minutes. Add the basil for the last 5 minutes.

3. Cook the pasta in a pan of salted boiling water until al dente. Add around 200 ml of the pasta water to the beef mince to form a soup-like consistency. Drain the pasta. Add it to the sauce.

4. To serve, ladle the soup into warmed bowls and top with the grated cheese.

# Fusilli with minced beef

SERVES: 4 | PREP TIME: 15 MINUTES | COOKING TIME: 30 MINUTES

## INGREDIENTS

2 tbsp olive oil

1 onion, diced

2 carrots, diced

2 cloves of garlic, minced

175 ml / 6 fl. oz / ⅔ cup red wine

100 g / 3 ½ oz cherry tomatoes, chopped

300 g / 10 ½ oz beef mince

300 g / 10 ½ oz fusilli

150 g / 5 ¼ oz burrata cheese

a small bunch of basil, finely chopped

## METHOD

1. In a sauté pan, heat the oil over a medium heat. Add the onion and carrot. Fry for 5 minutes until softened. Add the garlic to the pan and cook for a further minute. Pour the wine into the pan and cook until reduced by half in volume.

2. Add the cherry tomatoes to the pan and cook for 2-3 minutes until starting to break down. Add the beef and break up into smaller pieces. Season then cover and cook for 8-10 minutes.

3. Cook the pasta in a pan of boiling water as per the packet instructions. Drain and add to the beef pan. Mix through to coat the pasta with the sauce

4. Tear the burrata cheese into pieces. Place on top of the pasta in the pan, leave until starting to melt

5. Spoon the pasta onto serving plates and garnish with the finely chopped basil.

# Spaghetti and meatballs

SERVES: 4 | PREP TIME: 20 MINUTES | COOKING TIME: 25 MINUTES

## INGREDIENTS

300 g / 10 ½ oz beef mince

200 g / 7 oz pork mince

1 egg, beaten

o g / 1 ¾ oz / ½ cup Parmesan cheese, finely grated

1 tsp fennel seeds, crushed

a handful of fresh basil leaves, chopped

salt and freshly ground black pepper

2 tbsp olive oil

1 onion, diced

1 red pepper, diced

1 clove of garlic, minced

125 ml / 4 ½ fl. oz / ½ cup red wine

400 g / 14 oz / 14 oz canned plum tomatoes

a handful of basil leaves, chopped

250 g / 9 oz spaghetti

## METHOD

1. Place the first six ingredients in a large mixing bowl and season. Using your hands, mix and form into balls around the size of a golf ball.

2. Heat half the oil in a pan over a medium heat. Add the onion and pepper and cook for 5 minutes. Add the garlic. Cook for another minute.

3. Turn up the heat and add the wine. Allow to reduce by around half then turn the heat down and add the tomatoes and juice. Cook for 8-10 minutes. Add the basil leaves and season.

4. Heat the remaining oil in a frying pan and cook the meatballs for 2-3 minutes to brown the outside. Add them to the sauce for 10 minutes.

5. Cook the spaghetti as per the packet instructions, drain and set aside. To serve, add the pasta to plates and top with the meatballs and sauce.

# Spinach, ham and cheese ravioli

SERVES: 2-4 | PREP TIME: 40 MINUTES | COOKING TIME: 10 MINUTES

## INGREDIENTS

75 g / 2 ½ oz spinach, washed

300 g / 10 ½ oz / 2 cups pasta grade flour

a pinch of salt

4 large eggs

250 g / 9 oz ricotta

1 lemon, zested

300 g / 10 ½ oz buffalo mozzarella

2 slices cooked ham, chopped

25 g pine nuts

25 g Parmesan cheese, grated

2 tbsp extra virgin olive oil

## METHOD

1. Cook the spinach and drain on kitchen paper. Place into a blender and whizz into a puree.

2. Add the flour and salt to a mixing bowl. Make a well in the centre and add 3 eggs and the spinach puree. Incorporate the flour into the eggs and spinach using a fork until a dough forms. It should be sticky but not too wet, add more flour if needed or water if too dry.

3. Turn out onto a floured surface and knead for 10 minutes until you have a smooth and elastic dough. Roll into a ball and wrap in cling film before refrigerating for 20 minutes.

4. Using a pasta machine, roll out the dough into two long sheets around 2mm in thickness. Mix the ricotta with the lemon zest and season.

5. Slice the mozzarella. Place it onto one of the pasta sheets at regular intervals leaving space between each piece to form the ravioli. Top with some of the ricotta mix, chopped ham and pine nuts.

6. Beat the remaining egg and brush around the cheese, place the second pasta sheet on top and press around the filling to remove any air. Use a pasta cutter or knife to cut into rectangles. Repeat until all the filling is used.

7. Bring a pan of water to the boil and gently drop the ravioli into the water. Cook for around 1-2 minutes before draining and serving with a drizzle of oil and grated Parmesan cheese.

# Penne with beef ragu

SERVES: 4 | PREP TIME: 15 MINUTES | COOKING TIME: 45 MINUTES

## INGREDIENTS

2 tbsp olive oil

1 tbsp butter

1 onion, diced

2 carrots, grated

2 celery sticks, sliced

2 cloves of garlic, minced

1 tbsp tomato puree

500 g / 1 lb 1 oz beef mince

1 tsp dried oregano

5 sprigs of thyme

200 ml / 7 fl. oz / ¾ cup beef stock

400 g / 14 oz penne, cooked

150 g / 5 ¼ oz / 1 ½ cups mozzarella cheese, grated

## METHOD

1. Heat the oil and butter in a heavy pan with a lid over a medium heat, then add the onion. Cook for 2 minutes then add the carrot and celery. Place the lid on. Cook for 6-8 minutes.

2. Add the garlic and stir through for 1 minute, followed by the tomato puree. Add the beef and brown the meat for around 5 minutes.

3. Add the herbs and the beef stock. Bring up to a boil and then lower to a simmer and place the lid on top. Leave to cook on a gentle simmer for at least 30 minutes, season to taste.

4. Once the beef is ready, serve on warmed plates with the cooked penne and sprinkle over the grated cheese.

# Asian pork with tagliatelle

SERVES: 2 | PREP TIME: 15 MINUTES | COOKING TIME: 15 MINUTES

## INGREDIENTS

2 tbsp soy sauce

1 tsp Chinese five spice

1 tsp toasted sesame oil

1 lime, juice and zest

1 tsp honey

300 g / 10 ½ oz diced pork

150 g / 5 ¼ oz tagliatelle

3 spring onions (scallions), sliced

2 tsp black sesame seeds

## METHOD

1. Combine the soy, five spice, sesame oil, lime and honey in a large bowl.

2. Add the pork to the marinade and mix to coat the meat. Cover and leave to marinade for 10 minutes.

3. Heat a non-stick frying pan over a medium-high heat. Once hot, add the pork and stir-fry for 12-15 minutes until firm and cooked through.

4. At the same time, cook the pasta as per the packet instructions.

5. Add the pasta to the pork and mix through to coat the pasta in the sauce. Add a splash of the pasta water if the sauce is too thick.

6. Mix through the spring onions before adding to serving plates. Scatter over the sesame seeds.

# Pappardelle with prosciutto

SERVES: 2 | PREP TIME: 5 MINUTES | COOKING TIME: 15 MINUTES

## INGREDIENTS

150 g / 5 ¼ oz pappardelle
250 ml / 9 fl. oz / 1 cup double (heavy) cream
1 egg, beaten
100 g / 3 ½ oz / 1 cup Parmesan, grated
sea salt and freshly ground black pepper
150 g / 5 ¼ oz prosciutto, sliced

## METHOD

1. Cook the pasta as per the packet instructions. Drain and return to the pan.

2. In a jug or bowl, combine the cream, egg, Parmesan and season with the salt and black pepper.

3. While the pasta is still warm, place back onto the heat and pour the cream mixture into the pan. Quickly mix through the pasta to coat.

4. Mix the sliced ham through the pasta and serve on warmed plates.

# Conchiglie stuffed with beef

SERVES: 4-6 | PREP TIME: 15 MINUTES | COOKING TIME: 45 MINUTES

## INGREDIENTS

2 tbsp olive oil

1 onion, diced

2 carrots, diced

2 cloves of garlic, minced

175 ml / 6 fl. oz / ⅔ cup red wine

300 g / 10 ½ oz beef mince

400 g / 14 oz canned chopped tomatoes

400 g / 14 oz conchiglie

100 g / 3 ½ oz / 1 cup Parmesan cheese, grated

## METHOD

1. In a sauté pan, heat the oil over a medium heat. Add the onion and carrot and fry for around 5 minutes. Add the garlic to the pan and cook for a further minute. Pour the wine into the pan and cook until reduced by half in volume.

2. Add the beef and brown and break up into smaller pieces. Add the tomatoes and season before covering and cooking for 30 minutes.

3. Cook the pasta as per the packet instructions, drain and set aside.

4. Spoon the cooked beef into the pasta shells and add to individual serving plates. Spoon over any remaining sauce and top with grated cheese.

# Spaghetti and bacon fritters

SERVES: 4 | PREP TIME: 15 MINUTES | COOKING TIME: 10 MINUTES

## INGREDIENTS

200 g / 6 ½ oz / ¾ cup spaghetti

4 rashers bacon or pancetta, finely chopped

2 cloves of garlic, finely chopped

1 tbsp parsley, finely chopped

2 eggs

1 additional egg yolk

3 tbsp Parmesan, grated

3 tbsp olive oil

## METHOD

1. Cook the pasta in boiling water according to the packet instructions.

2. Cook the bacon in 1 tablespoon of oil until cooked. Mix together the garlic, parsley, eggs and Parmesan then stir into the bacon.

3. Drain the pasta and leave to cool, then roughly chop into shorter lengths.

4. Heat 2 tablespoons of oil in a pan (the bacon one for preference) and then spoon dollops of the spaghetti mixture into the pan.

5. Fry until crisp on both sides. Serve hot.

# Linguine with tomato and chicken

SERVES: 2 | PREP TIME: 15 MINUTES | COOKING TIME: 30 MINUTES

## INGREDIENTS

2 tbsp olive oil

1 onion, diced

1 clove of garlic, minced

100 g / 3 ½ oz vine ripened tomatoes, chopped

125 ml / 4 ½ fl. oz / ½ cup red wine

a handful of fresh basil chopped

150 g / 5 ¼ oz linguine

120 g / 4 ¼ oz chicken breast, diced

sea salt and cracked black pepper

## METHOD

1. Heat half the oil in a saucepan over a medium heat. Add the onion and cook for a couple of minutes until soft and translucent. Add the garlic and tomatoes to the pan and cook uncovered for a minute.

2. Add the wine to the pan and allow to reduce for a couple of minutes before covering and turning down the heat. Cook for 12-15 minutes or until the tomatoes have broken down. Add the basil to the sauce and blend the sauce using a hand blender until smooth. Cover and keep warm.

3. Place the pasta into a pan of boiling salted water and cook as per the packet instructions, drain and set aside.

4. Heat the remaining oil in a frying pan over a medium heat. Once hot, add the chicken to the pan and fry for 12-15 minutes until cooked through, season with salt and pepper.

5. Add the pasta and a spoonful of sauce to the chicken pan and mix to combine.

6. Serve on warmed plates and top with an additional spoonful of tomato sauce.

# Veal and pasta

SERVES: 2 | PREP TIME: 15 MINUTES | COOKING TIME: 15 MINUTES

## INGREDIENTS

2 veal escalopes, approx. 150 g / 5 ¼ oz each

2 free-range eggs

2 tbsp plain (all-purpose) flour

200 g / 7 oz / 1 ⅓ cups panko breadcrumbs, lightly crushed

25 g butter

2 tbsp olive oil

sea salt and freshly ground black pepper

pasta, to serve

## METHOD

1. Start by gently flattening out the veal by placing between two sheets of cling film and hitting with a rolling pin. Be careful to not break the meat, you just want to flatten it a little.

2. Beat the eggs and place into a bowl.

3. Place the flour onto a plate and season with salt and freshly ground black pepper.

4. Place the breadcrumbs onto another plate.

5. Take the veal and dip it first into the flour, then the egg and finally the breadcrumbs. Ensure that the meat is completely coated and shake off any excess.

6. Heat the butter and oil in a frying pan over a medium high heat. Once hot add the breaded veal and fry for around 5-8 minutes on each side until golden brown in colour.

7. Remove from the pan and place onto kitchen paper to drain.

8. Serve with some simple pasta drizzled with olive oil.

# Penne with cream and ham

SERVES: 1 | PREP TIME: 5 MINUTES | COOKING TIME: 15 MINUTES

## INGREDIENTS

80 g / 2 ¾ oz penne

100 ml / 3 ½ fl. oz / ½ cup double (heavy) cream

100 g / 3 ½ oz diced ham

25 g / 1 oz Parmesan cheese, grated

salt and cracked black pepper

2 tbsp fresh parsley, chopped

## METHOD

1. Cook the pasta in a pan of salted boiling water as per the packet instructions.

2. Once cooked, drain the pasta and return to the saucepan.

3. Add the cream, ham and cheese to the pan and mix until you have a thick creamy sauce. Season with salt and black pepper to taste before mixing though the parsley.

4. Serve in a warmed bowl and garnish with additional parsley and more cheese, if desired.

# Fusilli bucati with prosciutto

SERVES: 1 | PREP TIME: 10 MINUTES | COOKING TIME: 15 MINUTES

## INGREDIENTS

80 g / 2 ¾ oz fusilli bucati

50 g / 1 ¾ oz / ⅓ cup frozen peas

100 g / 3 ½ oz diced prosciutto

25 g / 1 oz Parmesan cheese, grated

salt and cracked black pepper

## METHOD

1. Cook the pasta in a pan of salted boiling water as per the packet instructions, add the peas to the pan for the last 5 minutes.

2. Once cooked, drain the pasta and peas before returning to the saucepan.

3. Stir the diced ham through the pasta.

4. Serve in a warmed bowl and garnish with the grated cheese and season with salt and pepper.

# Tagliatelle with sausage meatballs

SERVES: 2 | PREP TIME: 20 MINUTES | COOKING TIME: 20 MINUTES

## INGREDIENTS

250 g / 9 oz sausage meat

1 tsp oregano, dried

1 tsp sage, dried

1 tsp onion salt

1 clove of garlic, minced

1 tbsp breadcrumbs

50 g / 1 ¾ oz / ½ cup Parmesan cheese, grated

1 tbsp olive oil

120 g / 4 ¼ oz tagliatelle

150 ml / 5 ¼ fl. oz / ⅔ cup double (heavy) cream

## METHOD

1. In a mixing bowl, combine the sausage meat with the herbs, salt, garlic, breadcrumbs and a third of the cheese. Mix together with your hands until fully combined and form into balls roughly the size of a golf ball.

2. Heat the oil in a frying pan over a medium heat and add the meatballs. Fry them turning occasionally to brown on all sides.

3. At the same time, cook the pasta as per the packet instructions, drain well and set aside.

4. Once the meatballs have been cooking for around 12 minutes and are cooked through add the pasta to the pan along with the cream and remaining cheese. Mix through until the pasta is coated in the creamy sauce.

5. Divide between two warmed plates to serve and season with salt and black pepper.

# Penne with pork stew

SERVES: 4 | PREP TIME: 20 MINUTES | COOKING TIME: 40 MINUTES

## INGREDIENTS

400 g / 14 oz pork shoulder, cubed

2 tbsp olive oil

1 tbsp plain (all-purpose) flour

1 onion diced

1 clove of garlic, minced

150 g / 5 ¼ oz mushrooms, diced

400 g / 14 oz pork shoulder, cubed

400 ml / 13 ½ fl. oz / 1 ⅔ cups beef stock

several sprigs of thyme

350 g / 12 ¼ oz penne

a handful of chives, chopped

## METHOD

1. In a large casserole pan, add the oil and place onto a medium high heat. Add the pork to the pan and quickly brown for 2-3 minutes. Remove from the pan using a slotted spoon, and place onto a plate and dust with the flour.

2. Lower the heat a little and add the onions to the pan. Fry for 2-3 minutes before adding the garlic and mushrooms. Cook for a further couple of minutes before adding the stock and thyme to the pan. Reduce the heat to a simmer and stir the pork back into the pan, cover and cook for 30 minutes.

3. Cook the penne in a pan of boiling water for 10 minutes so that it is still slightly firm.

4. Drain the pasta and add to the pan with the pork, stir through and leave to cook in the sauce for a further 3-5 minutes until the pasta is cooked and the sauce reduced.

5. Season with salt and black pepper to taste before spooning into serving plates and garnishing with chopped chives.

## Cook's Corner

### Perfect Pasta

# Fish dishes

# Spaghetti with mussels

SERVES: 4 | PREP TIME: 15 MINUTES | COOKING TIME: 30 MINUTES

## INGREDIENTS

500 g / 1 lb / 2 cups spaghetti

500 g / 1 lb / 2 cups mussels, cleaned

2 tbsp olive oil

1 shallot, finely chopped

2 cloves of garlic, sliced

400 g / 14 oz / 2 cups chopped tomatoes

1 tbsp basil, chopped

## METHOD

1. Cook the pasta according to the packet instructions then drain well.

2. Place the mussels in a pan with a little water. Cook over a medium heat for 5 minutes. Drain in a colander over a bowl. Leave to cool.

3. Once cool, remove the mussel meat from the shells, reserving a few for decoration.

4. Heat the olive oil in a pan. Cook the shallot and garlic. Add the tomatoes and a little of the mussel cooking liquor. Leave to simmer for 10 minutes. Add the mussels to the sauce then toss with the spaghetti. Stir in the basil.

5. Serve decorated with the reserved shells.

# Pasta with prawns and coconut milk

SERVES: 2 | PREP TIME: 10 MINUTES | COOKING TIME: 15 MINUTES

## INGREDIENTS

200 g / 6 ½ oz / ¾ cup spirali pasta

200 ml / 6 ¾ fl. oz / 1 cup coconut milk

1 stalk lemongrass, crushed

1 lime, grated zest

200 g / 7 oz / ⅔ cup raw prawns (shrimps), shelled

1 tbsp basil, chopped

## METHOD

1. Cook the pasta according to the packet instructions. Drain and toss with a little oil.

2. Meanwhile heat the coconut milk in a pan and add the lemongrass and lime zest and leave to simmer for 5 minutes to infuse.

3. Add the prawns and leave until they turn pink, then stir in the basil and season.

4. Fish out the lemongrass stalk.

5. Toss through the pasta and serve.

73

# Tuna spaghetti

SERVES: 2 | PREP TIME: 10 MINUTES | COOKING TIME: 20 MINUTES

## INGREDIENTS

150 g / 5 ¼ oz spaghetti

1 tbsp olive oil

1 onion, diced

1 can tuna, drained

100 g / 3 ½ oz chestnut mushrooms, sliced

200 g / 7 oz passata

a small bunch of fresh basil, chopped

## METHOD

1. Cook the spaghetti in a pan of salted water as per the packet instructions, drain and set aside.

2. Heat the oil in a pan over a medium heat. Add the onion and cook for 3-4 minutes until softened.

3. Add the tuna to the pan and fry for 2-3 minutes. Add the mushrooms and cook for a further couple of minutes.

4. Pour the passata into the pan and cook for around 5 minutes.

5. Add the pasta to the pan to warm through, mixing to coat it fully in the sauce. Season well.

6. Place the pasta onto serving plates. Top with the chopped basil.

# Tagliatelle with salmon and sun-dried tomatoes

SERVES: 4 | PREP TIME: 5 MINUTES | COOKING TIME: 4 MINUTES

## INGREDIENTS

500 g / 1 lb 2 oz fresh tagliatelle pasta

4 tbsp olive oil

200 g / 7 oz / ¾ cup smoked salmon

100 g / 3 ½ oz / ½ cup sun-dried tomatoes

1 tbsp chervil, chopped

## METHOD

1. Cook the tagliatelle in boiling salted water according to the packet instructions.

2. Drain, reserving a small amount of the water, and toss with half the olive oil.

3. Cut the salmon into strips and tear the tomatoes into pieces. Place in a bowl with the chopped chervil and the remaining oil.

4. Toss with the pasta, adding a little of the reserved water to lubricate the sauce.

5. Season with salt and pepper and serve.

# Linguine with salmon and courgette

SERVES: 4 | PREP TIME: 10 MINUTES | COOKING TIME: 15 MINUTES

## INGREDIENTS

500 g / 1 lb 2 oz / 2 cups linguine

2 fillets smoked salmon, skin removed

2 courgettes (zucchini)

2 tbsp butter

200 ml / 7 fl. oz / ¾ cup double (heavy) cream

½ lemon, grated zest and juiced

1 tbsp basil, chopped

## METHOD

1. Cook the pasta in boiling salted water according to the packet instructions. Drain and toss with a little oil. Keep warm.

2. Meanwhile, gently flake the salmon into bite-sized pieces.

3. Slice the courgettes lengthways then cut into ribbons with a vegetable peeler.

4. Heat the butter in a pan and cook the courgettes for 2-3 minutes until just tender.

5. Stir in the cream, lemon zest and juice, basil, and then the salmon, stirring carefully. Season with salt and pepper

6. Toss with the linguine and serve.

# Ravioli with creamy lobster sauce

SERVES: 4 | PREP TIME: 1 HOUR | COOKING TIME: 5 MINUTES

## INGREDIENTS

500 g / 1lb 2 oz pasta dough

### FOR THE FILLING:

meat from 2 large crabs

200 g / 7 oz raw prawns (shrimps), shelled

75 ml / 3 fl. oz / ½ cup double (heavy) cream

1 tbsp chervil, chopped

1 egg, beaten

### FOR THE SAUCE:

800 ml / 1 pint 9 fl. oz lobster bisque

2 tomatoes, finely chopped

3 tbsp double (heavy) cream

½ lemon, juiced

1 handful chervil leaves

## METHOD

1. Place the prawns and cream in a food processor and blend to a puree. Mix with the crab meat and chervil.

2. Lay a sheet of pasta onto a floured work surface and place 1 teaspoon of the mixture at intervals along the sheet, leaving a 6 cm gap between each mound. Brush around each mound with a little beaten egg.

3. Top with the second sheet of pasta and press down lightly around each mound. Cut out or stamp out with a cutter and lay on a baking tray.

4. Heat the lobster bisque in a pan and allow to reduce to an intensity of flavour you like. Stir in the cream, tomatoes and a little lemon juice. Adjust the seasoning to taste.

5. Cook the ravioli in boiling salted water for 2 minutes until they float, then remove with a slotted spoon and drain on kitchen paper.

6. Serve with the hot sauce and garnish with chervil.

# Pasta with pesto and salmon

SERVES: 4 | PREP TIME: 10 MINUTES | COOKING TIME: 15 MINUTES

## INGREDIENTS

500 g / 1 lb / 2 cups penne pasta
2 tbsp olive oil
1 courgette (zucchini), thinly sliced
2 salmon steaks, cooked
handful black olives, pitted and chopped
2 tomatoes, finely chopped
4 tbsp pesto

## METHOD

1. Cook the pasta in boiling salted water according to the packet instructions. Drain, reserving a little of the cooking water.

2. Meanwhile heat the oil in a pan and cook the courgette until tender.

3. Flake the salmon into large chunks and mix with the chopped olives and tomatoes. Stir in the courgettes.

4. Add to the pan with the drained pasta, the pesto and a little cooking water to loosen the sauce.

5. Season with salt and pepper and serve.

# Tagliatelle with sea urchins

SERVES: 4 | PREP TIME: 5 MINUTES | COOKING TIME: 10 MINUTES

## INGREDIENTS

500 g / 1 lb 2 oz / 2 cups tagliatelle

2 tbsp olive oil

2 shallots, finely chopped

2 cloves of garlic, finely sliced

100 g / 4 oz sea urchin meat

½ bunch parsley, chopped

juice of ½ lemon

salt and pepper

## METHOD

1. Cook the pasta in boiling salted water according to the packet instructions.

2. Drain, reserving a little of the water and toss with oil.

3. Meanwhile, heat the oil in a pan and gently sweat the shallots and garlic.

4. Add the sea urchin meat and parsley. Toss well, then stir through the pasta and 2 tablespoons of cooking water.

5. Adjust the seasoning and squeeze over the lemon juice, if desired.

# Seafood lasagne

SERVES: 6 | PREP TIME: **30 MINUTES** | COOKING TIME: **50 MINUTES**

## INGREDIENTS

1 kg / 2 lbs / 4 cups mixed raw seafood

12 raw prawns (shrimps), shelled

12 sheets of lasagne, pre-cooked

5 tbsp olive oil

2 onions, peeled and chopped

1 tbsp butter

1 tbsp flour

400 ml / 13 ½ fl. oz / 1 ½ cups milk

1 bay leaf

nutmeg, grated to taste

a pinch of cayenne pepper

## METHOD

1. Heat half the oil in a pan and add the onion, seafood and prawns. Cook gently for 10-15 minutes.

2. In another pan, heat the butter and when foaming, stir in the flour to make a paste.

3. Whisk in the milk a little at a time. Add the bay leaf and a little nutmeg then continue whisking for 10 minutes until the sauce is smooth and thick. Season well and add a pinch of cayenne.

4. Preheat the oven to 190°C (170° fan) / 375F / gas 5.

5. Lightly oil a baking dish and place 4 lasagne sheets in the bottom.

6. Spoon over a third of the seafood, then some of the béchamel and repeat twice more, finishing with a layer of lasagne.

7. Pour over the remaining béchamel sauce and cook in the oven for about 30 minutes.

8. Leave to rest for 10 minutes before serving.

# Farfalle with scampi

SERVES: 4 | PREP TIME: 5 MINUTES | COOKING TIME: 12 MINUTES

## INGREDIENTS

500 g / 1 lb 2 oz / 2 cups farfalle pasta

2 tbsp butter

1 shallot, finely chopped

1 clove garlic, finely chopped

200 g / 7 oz cup raw shelled prawns

1 shot whisky

250 ml / 9 fl oz / 1 cup double (heavy) cream

salt and pepper

1 bunch chives, finely chopped

## METHOD

1. Cook the pasta in boiling water according to the packet instructions. Drain and toss with a little oil.

2. Meanwhile, heat the butter in a pan and sweat the shallot and garlic without colouring.

3. Add the prawns and fry briskly, adding the whisky and allowing it to evaporate.

4. Pour in the cream, season and cook until the prawns are just pink.

5. Toss the pasta with the sauce, sprinkling with chopped chives to serve.

# Seafood spaghetti

SERVES: 4 | PREP TIME: 15 MINUTES | COOKING TIME: 15-20 MINUTES

## INGREDIENTS

500 g / 1 lb / 2 cups spaghetti

2 tbsp olive oil

1 shallot, finely chopped

2 cloves garlic, finely chopped

1 pinch dried chilli (chili) flakes

800 g / 1 ¾ lbs / 4 cups chopped tomatoes

2 sprigs thyme

200 g / 7 oz / ⅔ cup raw prawns (shrimps), shelled

8 scallops, sliced in half horizontally

250 g / 9 oz / 1 cup mussels, cleaned

## METHOD

1. Cook the pasta in boiling salted water according to the packet instructions. Heat the oil in a pan. Sweat the shallot and garlic with chilli flakes without colouring.

2. Add the tomatoes with a splash of water and simmer for 10 minutes. Drain the pasta then toss with a little oil.

3. Cook the mussels in a separate pan with a splash of water for 5 minutes until they have opened. Discard any that remain closed.

4. Drain over a bowl to catch the cooking juices. Remove the meat from the mussels once cool.

5. Add the thyme, prawns and scallops to the tomato mixture and leave to cook until the prawns are pink and the scallops just opaque.

6. Add the mussels and a little of their cooking juice and season. Toss the spaghetti through the sauce and serve.

# Smoked salmon and pasta salad

SERVES: 4 | PREP TIME: 10 MINUTES | COOKING TIME: 12 MINUTES

### INGREDIENTS

300 g / 10 ½ oz / 1 ¼ cups penne pasta or similar

200 g / 7 oz / ¾ cup smoked salmon

4 spring onions (scallions), finely chopped

4 tbsp watercress, chopped

6 tbsp extra virgin olive oil

1 lemon, grated zest and juice

cornichons, to decorate

### METHOD

1. Cook the pasta in boiling salted water according to the packet instructions.

2. Drain, toss with a little oil and leave to cool.

3. Cut the salmon into fine strips and place in a bowl with onions and watercress. Add the pasta.

4. Whisk together the oil, lemon zest and juice and season.

5. Toss the salad with the dressing and serve immediately decorated with cornichons.

# Linguine with lobster

SERVES: **4** | PREP TIME: **5 MINUTES** | COOKING TIME: **20 MINUTES**

## INGREDIENTS

500 g / 1 lb / 2 cups linguine

2 tbsp butter

1 shallot, finely chopped

1 clove garlic, finely chopped

400 g / 14 oz / 2 cups chopped tomatoes

2 sprigs thyme

meat from 1 cooked lobster

## METHOD

1. Heat the butter in a pan and sweat the shallot and garlic without colouring.

2. Add the tomatoes with a splash of water and thyme and leave to simmer for 10 minutes.

3. Cook the pasta in boiling salted water according to the packet instructions.

4. Drain and toss with a little oil.

5. Slice the lobster into chunks and toss through the sauce to heat up. Adjust the seasoning to taste.

6. Toss the linguine with the sauce and serve.

89

# Tagliatelle with tuna

SERVES: 4 | PREP TIME: 5 MINUTES | COOKING TIME: 25 MINUTES

## INGREDIENTS

500 g / 1 lb 2 oz / 2 cups tagliatelle

3 tbsp olive oil

3-4 red peppers, roughly chopped

salt and pepper

375 g / 13 oz cans tuna in olive oil, drained

½ bunch basil, chopped

## METHOD

1. Preheat the oven to 200°C (180° fan) / 400F / gas 6.

2. Roast the peppers in oil and seasoning for about 20 minutes or until soft and sweet.

3. Cook the pasta in boiling salted water according to the packet instructions. Drain, reserving a little of the cooking water then tip into a bowl.

4. Toss with the roasted peppers, a little of the roasting juices and a tablespoon of cooking water.

5. Flake in the tuna and basil and season then serve.

# Lumaconi with salmon

SERVES: 2 | PREP TIME: 5 MINUTES | COOKING TIME: 15 MINUTES

## INGREDIENTS

500g / 1 lb / 2 cups lumaconi or other giant shell pasta

300ml / 10 fl oz / 1 ¼ cups double (heavy) cream

60g / 2 oz / ¼ cup salmon roe

¼ lemon, grated zest

1 tbsp chives, finely chopped

## METHOD

1. Cook the pasta in boiling salted water according to the packet instructions.

2. Meanwhile heat the cream gently with the salmon roe, zest and chives.

3. Season with salt and pepper.

4. Drain the pasta and toss with the sauce gently.

5. Serve immediately.

# Salmon pasta triangles with dill

SERVES: 4-6 | PREP TIME: 35 MINUTES | COOKING TIME: 7 MINUTES

CHILLING TIME: 30 MINUTES

## INGREDIENTS

### FOR THE PASTA:

500 g / 1 lb / 2 cups '00' flour
(Italian super-white flour)

4 eggs

500 g / 1 lb / 2 cups spinach leaves, wilted,
squeezed dry and cooled

### FOR THE FILLING:

3 tbsp butter

1 shallot, peeled and finely chopped

200 g / 7 oz / 1 cup smoked salmon, chopped

100 g / 3 ½ oz / ½ cup ricotta

### FOR THE SAUCE:

250 ml / 9 fl. oz / 1 cup double (heavy) cream

1 tbsp dill, chopped

## METHOD

1. Place the flour in a bowl, add the eggs and the spinach and combine until the dough comes together. Remove from the bowl and knead for 5 minutes.

2. Cover with film and chill for 30 minutes. Heat the butter in a pan and sweat the onion until soft. Stir into the ricotta with the salmon and season. Leave to cool.

3. Remove the pasta from the fridge. Using a pasta machine, roll out the dough into one even sheet. Cut into 10 cm (4 in) squares.

4. Lay on a floured surface and place 1 teaspoon of filling in the middle of each square. Moisten the edges with a little water then fold one corner over to make a triangle.

5. To cook bring a large pan of salted water to the boil and cook for 3-4 minutes. Remove carefully with a slotted spoon and drain on kitchen paper.

6. Gently warm the cream with a little seasoning and the dill and serve over the pasta.

# Seafood minestrone

SERVES: 2 | PREP TIME: 10 MINUTES | COOKING TIME: 35-40 MINUTES

## INGREDIENTS

1 tbsp olive oil

1 onion, peeled and finely chopped

1 carrot, peeled and finely chopped

1 celery stalk, peeled and chopped

2 tomatoes, finely chopped

1 ½ pints / 4 ¼ cups chicken stock

50 g / 1 ½ oz / ⅓ cup macaroni pasta

750 g / 1 ¼ lb / 3 cups mixed raw seafood,
such as prawns, scallops, mussels and squid

1 bunch parsley, chopped

½ lemon

salt and pepper

## METHOD

1. Heat the olive oil in a pan and sweat the onion, carrot and celery without colouring for 5 minutes.

2. Add the tomatoes and cook for a further 2 minutes.

3. Pour over the stock, bring to a simmer and add the pasta.

4. Cook for about 20 minutes until the pasta is tender.

5. Add the seafood and poach in the soup until the prawns turn pink, the scallops opaque and the mussels open. Discard any that remain closed.

6. Scatter over the parsley and adjust the seasoning.

# Conchiglie stuffed with crab

SERVES: 6 | PREP TIME: 20 MINUTES | COOKING TIME: 20 MINUTES

## INGREDIENTS

1 kg / 2 lb 4 oz / 4 cups giant conchiglie shells

300 g / 10 ½ oz crab meat

2 large bunches basil, chopped

75 g / 3 oz / ⅓ cup pine nuts

5 cloves of garlic, chopped

extra virgin olive oil

3 tomatoes, finely chopped

100 ml / 3 ½ fl oz / ½ cup vegetable stock

salt and pepper

## METHOD

1. Cook the pasta in boiling salted water according to the packet instructions. Drain and toss with olive oil.

2. Place the basil, garlic and pine nuts in a pestle and mortar and crush to make a paste then pour in enough oil to loosen.

3. Add the crab and tomatoes to the pesto and mix gently. Season. Preheat the oven to 150ºC (130º fan) / 300F / gas 2.

4. Stuff the pasta shells with the pesto mixture and place in a buttered baking dish.

5. Pour the stock into the bottom of the dish and cover with foil. Bake for 10 minutes then serve.

# Spinach tagliatelle with smoked trout

SERVES: 4 | PREP TIME: 5 MINUTES | COOKING TIME: 10 MINUTES

## INGREDIENTS

500 g / 1 lb / 2 cups spinach tagliatelle

300 g / 10 oz / 1 ¼ cups smoked trout

1 pack rocket (arugula)

1 tbsp olive oil

Parmesan shavings

## METHOD

1. Cook the pasta in boiling salted water according to the packet instructions.

2. Flake the trout and chop the rocket.

3. When cooked, drain the pasta, not too thoroughly, and toss with oil.

4. Stir through the trout and rocket.

5. Season and serve with Parmesan shavings.

# Pappardelle with mixed seafood

SERVES: 2 | PREP TIME: 10 MINUTES | COOKING TIME: 15 MINUTES

## INGREDIENTS

1 tbsp olive oil

1 shallot, diced

1 clove of garlic, minced

200 ml / 7 fl. oz / ¾ cup white wine

100 g / 3 ½ oz cherry tomatoes, quartered

225 g / 8 oz mixed shellfish, cooked

120 g / 4 ¼ oz fresh pappardelle

a small bunch of flat-leaved parsley, roughly torn

sea salt and cracked black pepper

## METHOD

1. Heat the oil in a pan with a lid over a medium heat. Add the shallot and garlic. Cook for 2-3 minutes until soft. Add the wine to the pan. Allow to reduce by half. Add most of the tomatoes and seafood, turn the heat down and cover.

2. Add the pasta to a pan of boiling water. Cook for around 3 minutes until tender. Add a ladle of the pasta water to the seafood pan, before draining and adding the pasta.

3. Toss the pasta into the sauce to coat, add the parsley to the pan and season.

4. Spoon into serving plates. Top with the reserved tomatoes.

# Black spaghetti with seafood

SERVES: 2 | PREP TIME: 15 MINUTES | COOKING TIME: 20 MINUTES

## INGREDIENTS

100 g / 3 ½ oz clams
150 g / 5 ¼ oz mussels
2 tbsp olive oil
1 shallot, diced
1 clove of garlic, minced
200 ml / 7 fl. oz / ¾ cup white wine
1 tbsp tomato puree
100 g / 3 ½ oz raw king prawns
100 g / 3 ½ oz squid rings
120 g / 4 ¼ oz black spaghetti
fresh basil, to garnish

## METHOD

1. Clean the clams and mussels in a bowl of water. Remove any with broken shells or that do not close when tapped. Rinse to remove dirt and grit.

2. Heat the oil in a pan over a mid-high heat. Fry the shallot and garlic for 1 minute. Add the clams, mussels and wine to the pan. Cook until the liquid has reduced by half before adding the tomato puree, prawns and squid. Place the lid on the pan. Turn down the heat. Cook for 10 minutes until the shellfish are open and prawns/squid are cooked.

3. In another pan, cook the spaghetti as per the packet instructions then add it to the seafood.

4. Spoon into bowls and garnish with the basil.

99

# Penne with spicy king prawns

SERVES: 2 | PREP TIME: 10 MINUTES | COOKING TIME: 20 MINUTES

## INGREDIENTS

180 g / 6 ¼ oz penne pasta

1 tbsp olive oil

1 onion, diced

2 cloves of garlic, minced

1 red chilli (chili), finely chopped

2 tbsp tomato puree

180 g / 6 ¼ oz raw king prawns

250 ml / 9 fl. oz / 1 cup red wine

25 g Parmesan cheese, grated

## METHOD

1. Cook the pasta as per the packet instructions.

2. As the pasta is cooking, heat the oil in a pan over mid-high heat. Add the onions. Fry for 4 minutes. Add the garlic and chilli. Cook for 1 more minute

3. Add the tomato puree and prawns to the pan. Stir then add the wine. Turn the heat up and let the alcohol cook off and reduce for 5 minutes. The prawns should be pink and cooked through

4. Drain the pasta and add some of the water from the saucepan to the prawns to loosen the sauce.

5. Add the pasta to the prawns and mix through, adding the cheese as you do so. Season to taste.

# Steamed mussels with spaghetti

SERVES: 2 | PREP TIME: 15 MINUTES | COOKING TIME: 15 MINUTES

## INGREDIENTS

300 g / 10 ½ oz fresh mussels

150 g / 5 ¼ oz spaghetti

1 tbsp olive oil

2 shallots, diced

2 cloves of garlic, minced

250 ml / 9 fl. oz / 1 cup white wine

2 tbsp tomato puree

a small bunch of flat-leaved parsley, chopped

## METHOD

1. Clean the mussels. Check for any which do not close when tapped. Discard these and any others with broken shells. Rinse to remove grit.

2. Cook the pasta as per the packet instructions.

3. Heat the oil in a pan with a lid. Add the shallots and garlic. Cook for 2 minutes. Add the mussels and shake the pan before pouring in the white wine. Cover and leave to cook for 5 minutes.

4. Drain the pasta and reserve a little of the water.

5. Stir the tomato puree into the mussels. Mix in the parsley. Serve the pasta in bowls topped with the cooked mussels and sauce.

# Tagliatelle with salmon and parsley

SERVES: 1 | PREP TIME: 10 MINUTES | COOKING TIME: 15 MINUTES

## INGREDIENTS

1 salmon fillet

1 clove of garlic, whole

1 lemon, juice and zest

1 tbsp olive oil

75 g / 2 ½ oz tagliatelle

a handful of flat-leaved parsley, chopped

## METHOD

1. Preheat the oven to 180°C (160°C fan) / 350F / gas 4.

2. Place the salmon in the centre of a large piece of foil. Add the garlic and drizzle over the lemon and oil before seasoning with salt and black pepper. Fold over the edges of the foil to make a parcel.

3. Place the salmon parcel onto a baking tray and cook in the hot oven for 12-15 minutes until cooked through. Remove and set aside.

4. Cook the pasta in a pan of salted boiling water as per the packet instructions, drain and set aside.

5. To serve, flake the salmon in a bowl with the juices from the cooking process. Mix with the pasta and parsley and toss to combine before placing onto a serving plate.

# Spaghetti vongole

SERVES: 2 | PREP TIME: 15 MINUTES | COOKING TIME: 15 MINUTES

## INGREDIENTS

500 g / 1 lb 1 oz fresh clams, scrubbed clean

200 g / 7 oz spaghetti

2 tbsp olive oil

1 shallot, diced

2 cloves of garlic, minced

50 g / 1 ¾ oz cherry tomatoes, halved

a small bunch of parsley, chopped

150 ml / 5 ¼ fl. oz / ⅔ cup white wine

a pinch of chilli (chili) flakes

sea salt and freshly ground black pepper

## METHOD

1. Place the clams into a bowl of water. Give any that are not already closed a tap (if they do not close, discard them).

2. Cook the pasta in pan of salted boiling water as per the packet instructions.

3. About 5 minutes before the pasta is ready heat the oil in a large saucepan over a medium heat. Add the shallot and garlic and cook for a minute until softened. Add the tomatoes and parsley followed by the clams, wine and chilli flakes. Put the lid on the pan and give it a shake. Do this a couple times for around 4 minutes.

4. Remove the lid and add the drained pasta to the pan. Mix together to coat the pasta in the juices from the clams and wine for a further minute or two.

5. Spoon into serving dishes with the sauce and serve with crusty bread. Take care to discard any clams that have not opened during cooking.

# Prawns with tagliatelle

SERVES: 2 | PREP TIME: 10 MINUTES | COOKING TIME: 15 MINUTES

## INGREDIENTS

100 g / 3 ½ oz tagliatelle

120 g / 4 ¼ oz raw king prawns

1 lemon, juice and zest

2 tbsp olive oil

50 g / 1 ¾ oz cherry tomatoes

½ green pepper, sliced

½ yellow pepper, sliced

50 g / 1 ¾ oz red leaf lettuce

## METHOD

1.  Cook the pasta as per the packet instructions. Once cooked, drain and set aside.

2.  Mix the prawns with the lemon and oil before seasoning with salt and black pepper.

3.  Heat the oil in a frying pan over a medium heat. Add the prawns and cook for 6-8 minutes until pink and firm to the touch. Add the tomatoes to the pan and cook for 2-3 minutes before adding the pasta. Stir the pasta through until warmed through.

4.  Mix the pasta with the raw peppers and place into serving plates before garnishing with the lettuce leaves.

## Cook's Corner

### Perfect Pasta

# Vegetable and herb dishes

# Penne with asparagus and tomatoes

SERVES: 1 | PREP TIME: 5 MINUTES | COOKING TIME: 15 MINUTES

## INGREDIENTS

75 g / 2 ½ oz penne pasta

1 tbsp tomato puree

75 g / 2 ½ oz asparagus tips

75 g / 2 ½ oz cherry tomatoes, halved

1 tbsp extra virgin olive oil

several sprigs of basil

sea salt and freshly ground black pepper

## METHOD

1. Cook the pasta in a pan of boiling water for 10-12 minutes until soft. Drain, reserving a little of the pasta water. Return the pasta to the pan and stir through the tomato puree, adding some of the reserved water to loosen the sauce.

2. Boil the asparagus in a pan of water for 8-10 minutes until tender. Drain and mix through the pasta.

3. Stir the halved cherry tomatoes through the pasta with the oil.

4. Add to warmed serving plates and garnish with basil sprigs and generously season with salt and black pepper.

# Vegetable lasagne

SERVES: 6-8 | PREP TIME: 20 MINS | COOKING TIME: 1 HOUR 30 MINS

## INGREDIENTS

1 tsp olive oil

1 large onion, diced

2 cloves of garlic, finely chopped

500 g / 1 lb 1 oz mushrooms, diced

2 aubergines (eggplant), cubed

1 tsp tomato puree

400 g / 14 oz can chopped tomatoes

a handful of fresh basil, chopped

1 litre / 35 fl. oz semi-skimmed milk

30 g unsalted butter

30 g plain (all-purpose) flour

30 g corn flour (corn starch)

75 g / 2 ½ oz / ¾ cup Parmesan cheese

200 g / 7 oz / 2 cups grated mozzarella

125 g / 4 ¼ oz buffalo mozzarella, sliced

250 g / 9 oz lasagne sheets

## METHOD

1. Preheat the oven to 180°C (160°C fan) / 350F / gas 4.

2. In a pan, heat the olive oil over a medium heat. Add the onions and cook for 5 minutes. Add the garlic and fry for a further minute.

3. Add the mushrooms and aubergine and fry for a further 5 minutes. Add the tomato puree to the pan and fry for a further minute. Pour in the tomatoes and bring to the boil before reducing to a simmer. Cover and cook for 30 minutes, adding the basil for the last 10 minutes.

4. Make the white sauce by combining the milk, butter, flour and cornflour in a saucepan. Gently heat, whisking continuously until thickened. Grate in the Parmesan cheese and season with salt and black pepper.

5. To make the lasagne, spoon a layer of the vegetable sauce into a rectangular ovenproof dish. Top with a layer of pasta followed by a layer of white sauce. Repeat until all the sauce has been used, finishing with a layer of white sauce. Top with grated cheese and slices of buffalo mozzarella.

6. Bake in the oven for 45 minutes until the top has browned and the pasta has softened.

7. Serve with a crisp salad.

# Spaghetti with mushrooms

SERVES: 2 | PREP TIME: 10 MINUTES | COOKING TIME: 15 MINUTES

## INGREDIENTS

1 tbsp olive oil

1 tsp butter

250 g / 9 oz mushrooms, sliced

1 clove of garlic, minced

125 ml / 4 ½ fl. oz / ½ cup Marsala

125 g / 4 ¼ oz spaghetti

25 g Parmesan cheese, grated

basil and tomatoes, to garnish

sea salt and cracked black pepper

## METHOD

1. Heat the olive oil in a frying pan over a medium-high heat and add the butter.

2. Once the butter is frothy, add the sliced mushrooms and cook for 8-10 minutes until they have started to colour. Add the mince, garlic and cook for a minute before adding the marsala. Continue to cook in the marsala until it has nearly completely reduced.

3. Cook the spaghetti in a pan of boiling water as per the packet instructions. Drain and add to the pan with the mushrooms, toss to combine the ingredients, seasoning as you do.

4. Spoon onto plates. Sprinkle over the grated cheese. Garnish with the basil and tomatoes.

# Courgetti spaghetti duo

SERVES: 2 | PREP TIME: 15 MINUTES | COOKING TIME: 5 MINUTES

## INGREDIENTS

a large bunch of basil, chopped

a large bunch of parsley, chopped

1 clove of garlic

25 g / 1 oz pine nuts

50 ml / 1 ¾ fl. oz / ¼ cup extra virgin olive oil

1 lemon, zest and juice

25 g Parmesan cheese, grated

300 g / 10 ½ oz courgetti or spiralized courgette (zucchini)

200 g / 7 oz spaghetti

75 g / 2 ½ oz cherry tomatoes, halved

## METHOD

1. Place the first seven ingredients into a blender and blend for 1 minute until combined. If a little thick, add some more oil. Season with salt and black pepper to taste.

2. Meanwhile, place the spaghetti into a pan of boiling water and cook according to the packet instructions. Drain then return to the pan.

3. Place the courgetti into a pan of boiling water and cook for around 1 minute until tender, drain then place the courgetti into the pan with the spaghetti.

4. Add a large spoonful of the pesto and the tomatoes to the pan. Mix to thoroughly coat the courgetti and spaghetti with the pesto.

5. Spoon into warmed serving bowls and garnish with any additional basil leaves. Any leftover pesto will keep in the refrigerator for 2-3 days.

# Pasta ramen

SERVES: 4 | PREP TIME: 20 MINUTES | COOKING TIME: 30 MINUTES

## INGREDIENTS

500 ml / 17 fl. oz / 2 cups vegetable stock
2 cloves of garlic, crushed
1 tsp Chinese five spice
2 tbsp soy sauce
1 tbsp fish sauce
2 limes, juiced
1 tsp chilli (chili) flakes
1 inch piece of root ginger, sliced
250 g / 9 oz fusilli bucatini
1 tsp baking soda
2 heads of broccoli, florets only
4 fresh duck egg yolks

## METHOD

1. In a stockpot, combine the first eight ingredients and heat to a gentle simmer. Cover and leave to cook for 15-20 minutes, taste to check seasoning.

2. Cook the fusilli in a pan of salted boiling water with the baking soda, taking care not to let it boil over. Once tender, drain and set aside.

3. Cook the broccoli in a pan of boiling water for 8-10 minutes until tender. Drain and set aside.

4. Place the pasta and broccoli into serving bowls and top up with the chicken stock mixture. Carefully place the egg yolk on top and serve.

# Squash ragu with penne

SERVES: 4 | PREP TIME: 15 MINUTES | COOKING TIME: 30 MINUTES

## INGREDIENTS

2 tbsp olive oil

1 tbsp butter

1 onion, diced

2 cloves of garlic, minced

1 tbsp tomato puree

500 g / 1 lb 1 oz butternut squash, diced

250 ml / 9 fl. oz / 1 cup vegetable stock

a handful of sage leaves, chopped

450 g / 1 lb penne

75 g / 2 ½ oz / ¾ cup pecorino cheese, grated

## METHOD

1. Heat the oil and butter in a heavy pan with a lid over a medium heat. Once the butter is frothing, add the onion with a pinch of salt. Place the lid on and cook for 6-8 minutes until softened.

2. Add the garlic and stir through for a minute until fragrant, followed by the tomato puree.

3. Add the diced squash and mix through for 2 minutes then add the stock. Bring to the boil then lower to a simmer and place the lid on top. Leave to cook on a gentle simmer for at least 30 minutes. Season to taste.

4. Cook the pasta as per the packet instructions, then drain. Mix into the butternut squash sauce.

5. Spoon onto warmed serving plates and top with the grated pecorino.

# Tortellini with tomato pesto

SERVES: 2 | PREP TIME: 10 MINUTES | COOKING TIME: 15 MINUTES

## INGREDIENTS

2 tbsp olive oil

100 g / 3 ½ oz cherry tomatoes

100 g / 3 ½ oz / ½ cup sundried tomatoes

a large bunch of basil, chopped

2 cloves of garlic

25 g / 1 oz / ¼ cup pine nuts

50 ml / 1 ¾ fl. oz / ¼ cup extra virgin olive oil

1 lemon, zest and juice

25 g Parmesan cheese, grated

250 g / 9 oz tortellini

## METHOD

1. Preheat the oven to 180°C (160°C fan) / 350F / gas 4. Drizzle the oil over the tomatoes and place into the oven and roast for 4-6 minutes until softened. Remove and set aside.

2. Combine the sundried tomatoes, basil, garlic, pine nuts, extra virgin olive oil, lemon and Parmesan cheese in a blender. Blend for 2-3 minutes until combined but still with a few chunks.

3. Mix the roast tomatoes into the sundried tomato pesto and season to taste.

4. Cook the tortellini in a pan of boiling water as per the packet instructions and drain.

5. Add the cooked tortellini to serving plates and top with the tomato pesto.

# Quail egg pasta salad

SERVES: 1 | PREP TIME: 10 MINUTES | COOKING TIME: 10 MINUTES

## INGREDIENTS

3 quail eggs

50 g / 1 ¾ oz farfalle

50 g / 1 ¾ oz rocket (arugula)

50 g / 1 ¾ oz cherry tomatoes, halved

a handful of basil leaves

1 tbsp olive oil

1 tbsp balsamic glaze

## METHOD

1. Place the eggs into a pan of water, bring to the boil and cook for 2 minutes. Drain and return to the pan and cover with cold water. Once cool enough to handle, peel and cut in half.

2. Cook the farfalle in a pan of salted boiling water as per the packet instructions. Drain and set aside to cool.

3. Combine the pasta, rocket, tomatoes and basil in a bowl. Drizzle with the oil and season with salt and black pepper. Toss to combine and add to a serving plate.

4. Arrange the eggs on the plate and drizzle over the balsamic glaze.

# Tomato and pasta soup

SERVES: 4 | PREP TIME: 15 MINUTES | COOKING TIME: 30-35 MINUTES

## INGREDIENTS

2 tbsp olive oil

1 onion, peeled and chopped

1 carrot, peeled and finely chopped

1 celery stalk, finely chopped

2 cloves of garlic, chopped

1 courgette, finely chopped

2 potatoes, peeled and finely chopped

400 g / 14 oz / 4 cups dried macaroni

400 g / 14 oz / 2 cups canned chopped tomatoes

1 l / 1 pint 16 fl. oz / 4 cups vegetable stock

salt and pepper

extra virgin olive oil

## METHOD

1. Cook the pasta as per the packet instructions.

2. Meanwhile, heat the oil in a pan and sweat the onion, carrot and celery without colouring.

3. Add the garlic and cook for 2 minutes until soft.

4. Add the courgettes and potatoes, stir and leave to soften for 10 minutes.

5. Pour in the tomatoes, crumble in a little of the chilli, then stir in the stock. Bring to a simmer and leave to cook for 20 minutes, until the vegetables are tender. Taste and adjust the seasoning.

6. Roughly mash the vegetables with a potato masher.

7. Drain and mix the boiled pasta into the soup. Serve drizzled with olive oil.

# Tagliatelle with green vegetables

SERVES: 4 | PREP TIME: 10 MINUTES | COOKING TIME: 1 HOUR

## INGREDIENTS

PASTA DOUGH:

600 g / 1 lb 5 oz / 4 cups '00' flour
(Italian super-white flour)

6 eggs or 12 egg yolks

FOR THE SAUCE:

2 tbsp butter

200 g / 7 oz / 2 cups broad beans, double podded

200 g / 7 oz / 2 cups peas

8 asparagus stalks, woody ends snapped off
and cut into short lengths

2 tbsp Parmesan, grated

## METHOD

1.  Tip the flour into a bowl, make a well in the centre and crack the eggs into it. Beat the eggs until smooth then mix together with the flour.

2.  Use your hands to bring the dough into a ball. Remove from the bowl. Knead for 10 minutes. Cover with film. Chill for 30 minutes.

3.  Roll the pasta out, with a pasta machine, to its thinnest setting, then use the tagliatelle setting to make the pasta shapes. Set aside.

4.  Boil the beans and peas in water for 4 minutes. Boil the pasta in water for 4 minutes then drain.

5.  Heat the butter in a pan and cook the vegetables for 3 minutes. Once the asparagus is tender, add the pasta and stir. Serve with Parmesan.

# Tricolore pasta salad

SERVES: 4 | PREP TIME: 15 MINUTES | COOKING TIME: 20 MINUTES

## INGREDIENTS

400 g / 14 oz / 3 ½ cups farfalle

300 g / 10 ½ oz / 2 cups cherry tomatoes

2 green peppers, roasted and cooled

1 tbsp basil, chopped

4 tbsp olive oil

2 tbsp red wine vinegar

1 ball buffalo mozzarella

## METHOD

1. Cook the pasta in boiling salted water according to the packet instructions.

2. Drain and toss with olive oil.

3. Meanwhile tip the tomatoes into a bowl with the peppers and drizzle with the olive oil, the vinegar and season.

4. Toss the cooked pasta with the tomatoes and peppers, adding more oil, if necessary, to lubricate. Adjust the seasoning.

5. Tear over the mozzarella and serve.

# Tagliatelle with creamy lemon sauce

SERVES: 4 | PREP TIME: 2 MINUTES | COOKING TIME: 5 MINUTES

## INGREDIENTS

500 g / 1 lb 2 oz / 2 cups fresh tagliatelle

250 ml / 9 fl. oz / 1 cup crème fraiche

1 lemon, grated zest and juiced

2 tbsp basil, chopped

salt and pepper

## METHOD

1. Cook the pasta in boiling salted water according to the packet instructions.

2. Warm the crème fraiche in a pan with the lemon zest and juice, basil and season with salt and pepper.

3. Toss the pasta in the sauce with a little of the pasta cooking water to loosen.

# Courgette lasagne

SERVES: 4 | PREP TIME: 25 MINUTES | COOKING TIME: 25 MINUTES

## INGREDIENTS

4 courgettes (zucchini)
2 tbsp olive oil
2 cloves garlic, chopped
300 g / 10 oz / 1 cup ricotta
4 tbsp Parmesan, grated
½ lemon, grated zest
8 lasagne sheets
300 g / 10 oz / 1 ¼ cups crème fraiche
2 handfuls Cheddar, grated
1 ball mozzarella, sliced

## METHOD

1. Preheat the oven to 180°C / 350F / gas 5.

2. Grate 2 of the courgettes and slice the remaining 2 thinly lengthways using a vegetable peeler.

3. Heat the olive oil in a pan and fry the garlic until soft. Stir in the grated courgette and allow to soften. Fold into the ricotta and 3 tablespoons of Parmesan, then add the lemon zest and season well.

4. Lay half the lasagne sheets in the bottom of a greased baking dish then spoon over half the filling. Place some of the courgette slices on top.

5. Top with the remaining lasagne sheets then repeat until all the ingredients are used up, finishing with a layer of sliced courgettes.

6. Whisk together the crème fraiche, Cheddar and remaining Parmesan. Loosen with a little milk if necessary then spoon over the top of the lasagne.

7. Lay slices of the mozzarella over and bake in the oven for 20-25 minutes until bubbling.

# Mushroom ravioli

SERVES: 6 | PREP TIME: 45 MINUTES | RESTING TIME: 30 MINUTES
COOKING TIME: 3 MINUTES

## INGREDIENTS

**FOR THE PASTA:**

500 g / 1 lb 2 oz / 3 ⅓ cups '00' flour

6 eggs

**FOR THE FILLING:**

3 tbsp butter

200 g / 7 oz / 2 ⅔ cup wild mushrooms,
brushed clean

150 g / 5 oz / 2 cups flat mushrooms, finely chopped

½ onion, peeled and finely chopped

2 tbsp Parmesan, grated

1 tbsp flat-leaved parsley, finely chopped

salt and pepper

**GARNISH:**

butter

Parmesan, grated

## METHOD

1. Place the flour in a bowl. Make a well in the centre. Crack the eggs into the well.

2. Beat the eggs, then draw in the flour until the dough comes together. Knead the dough for 5 minutes. Cover with film and rest for 30 minutes in the refrigerator.

3. Heat the butter and sweat the onion and mushrooms. Stir in the Parmesan and parsley and season.

4. Using a pasta machine, roll the dough into sheets 2 mm thick and around 10 cm wide. Lay on a floured surface.

5. Place 1 teaspoon of filling in the middle of the sheet at one end. Repeat all the way along at 5 cm intervals and then brush a little water in a circle, around each filling.

6. Place another sheet of pasta on top, then push the sheets together and around each mound of filling.

7. Cut the ravioli into shapes.

8. Bring a large pan of water to the boil and cook the ravioli for 3-4 minutes. Remove with a slotted spoon then toss with more butter and Parmesan to serve.

# Vegetarian lasagne

SERVES: 4 | PREP TIME: 2 HOURS | COOKING TIME: 40 MINUTES

## INGREDIENTS

150ml / 5 fl oz / ⅔ cup vegetable stock

12 lasagne sheets

2 tbsp vegetarian Parmesan, grated

FOR THE BOLOGNESE SAUCE:

1 tbsp butter

1 tbsp olive oil

1 onion, peeled and finely chopped

2 celery stalks, finely chopped

2 cloves garlic, finely chopped

2 carrots, finely chopped

500 g / 1 lb vegetarian mince substitute

120 ml / 4 fl. oz / ½ cup white wine

6 button mushrooms, finely chopped

400 g / 14 oz / 2 cups canned tomatoes

450 ml / 1 pint / 2 cups vegetable stock

FOR THE BÉCHAMEL SAUCE:

2 tbsp butter

2 tbsp plain (all-purpose) flour

700 ml / 1 ¼ pints / 2 ¾ cups milk

1 bay leaf

nutmeg, grated

## METHOD

1. To make the sauce, heat the butter and oil in a pan, add the chopped vegetables and cook for 10 minutes.

2. Add the vegetarian mince and the wine and stir for 5 minutes until it has been absorbed. Add the mushrooms so they blend in with the vegetarian mince.

3. Add the tomatoes and half the stock. Lower the heat and partially cover. Leave to simmer for 2 hours, adding more stock as it absorbs.

4. Meanwhile, to make the béchamel sauce, heat the butter in a pan and stir in the flour to make a paste.

5. Whisk in the milk, whisking until all the milk has been added. Add the bay leaf and simmer for 10 minutes, whisking until thick and smooth. Add a little nutmeg.

6. Preheat the oven to 190C / 375F / gas 5. Add 4 lasagne sheets then spread a third of the bolognese sauce in the bottom of a baking dish, then a quarter of the béchamel.

7. Repeat twice more, then cover the top layer of lasagne with béchamel and sprinkle over the vegetarian Parmesan.

8. Bake in the oven for about 40 minutes until the pasta is tender.

9. Leave to rest for 10 minutes before serving.

# Fettuccine with rosemary butter sauce

SERVES: 4 | PREP TIME: 5 MINUTES | COOKING TIME: 10 MINUTES

### INGREDIENTS

500 g / 1 lb 2 oz / 2 cups fettuccine pasta

100 g / 3 ½ oz / ½ cup butter

3 sprigs rosemary leaves, finely chopped

2 cloves garlic, finely chopped

4 tbsp Parmesan, grated, to serve

### METHOD

1. Cook the pasta in boiling salted water according to the packet instructions.

2. Drain, reserving a little of the cooking water, and toss with a little oil to prevent sticking.

3. Meanwhile heat the butter in a pan and gently fry the garlic and rosemary until soft.

4. Toss the pasta in the butter with 2-3 tablespoons of cooking water to emulsify the sauce.

5. Season and serve with grated Parmesan.

# Spaghetti in tomato sauce

SERVES: 4 | PREP TIME: 5 MINUTES | COOKING TIME: 12 MINUTES

## INGREDIENTS

500 g / 1 lb 2 oz / 4 ½ cups dried spaghetti

2 tbsp olive oil

2 cloves garlic, chopped

400 g / 14 oz / 2 cups chopped tomatoes

2 tbsp butter

2 tbsp Parmesan, grated to serve

## METHOD

1. Cook the pasta according to the packet instructions. Drain and toss with a little extra virgin olive oil and keep warm.

2. Heat the oil in a pan with the garlic for a few minutes.

3. When the garlic starts to sizzle, increase the heat and throw in the tomatoes. Immediately place a lid on and leave for a few minutes until the sizzling dies down.

4. Remove the lid, stir in the butter and season with salt and pepper.

5. Toss the spaghetti in the sauce and serve with grated Parmesan.

# Angel hair pasta with shallots and parsley sauce

SERVES: 4 | PREP TIME: 5 MINUTES | COOKING TIME: 5 MINUTES

## INGREDIENTS

500 g / 1 lb 2 oz / 2 cups angel hair pasta

4 tbsp butter

2 shallots, finely chopped

1 clove garlic, finely chopped

2 tbsp flat-leaved parsley, finely chopped

4 tbsp Parmesan, grated

## METHOD

1. Cook the pasta in boiling salted water according to the packet instructions.

2. Drain, toss with a little oil and keep warm.

3. Meanwhile, heat the butter in a pan and gently sweat the shallot and garlic without colouring.

4. Stir in the parsley, season and then toss with the pasta.

5. Serve with the Parmesan sprinkled over.

# Spaghetti with pesto and garlic

SERVES: 4 | PREP TIME: 5 MINUTES | COOKING TIME: 10 MINUTES

## INGREDIENTS

500 g / 1 lb / 2 cups spaghetti

FOR THE PESTO SAUCE:
small handful pine nuts
1 clove of garlic, peeled and chopped
3 big handfuls basil leaves, chopped
2 tbsp Parmesan, grated
extra virgin olive oil

## METHOD

1. Cook the pasta in boiling water according to the packet instructions. Drain, reserving a little of the water.

2. Make the pesto sauce, whizz the ingredients in a food processor until you have a rough paste or pound in a pestle and mortar. Drizzle in enough oil to make a loose sauce.

3. Toss the pasta in the pesto, loosening with a little cooking water.

4. Serve with extra Parmesan.

# Tortellini with spinach and cream

SERVES: 4-6 | PREP TIME: 1 HOUR 30 MINS | COOKING TIME: 10 MINS

## INGREDIENTS

FOR THE PASTA:

500 g / 1 lb 2 oz / 2 cups grade '00' flour

4 eggs

500 g / 1 lb 2 oz / 2 cups spinach leaves, wilted, squeezed dry and cooled

FOR THE FILLING:

3 tbsp butter

½ onion, peeled and finely chopped

1 clove garlic, finely chopped

500 g / 1 lb 2 oz / 2 cups spinach leaves

nutmeg, grated

100 g / 3 ½ oz / ½ cup ricotta

2 tbsp Parmesan, grated

1 tbsp flat-leaved parsley, chopped

FOR THE SAUCE:

250 ml / 9 fl. oz / 1 cup double cream

Parmesan, grated

## METHOD

1. Mix the pasta ingredients then knead with your hands for 5 minutes until smooth. Cover with film and chill for 30 minutes.

2. Heat the butter in a pan and sweat the onion and garlic. Add the spinach, wilt down then add the nutmeg. Stir in the ricotta, Parmesan and parsley and leave to cool.

3. Using a pasta machine, roll out the dough into one even sheet. Cut into 10 cm (4 in) squares.

4. Place 1 teaspoon of filling in the middle of each square, then fold one corner over to make a triangle.

5. Press the edges lightly together, bringing the corners of the triangle in together to make a circular shape.

6. To cook, bring a large pan of water to the boil and cook for 3-4 minutes. Remove with a slotted spoon and drain on kitchen paper.

7. Gently warm the cream with a little seasoning and serve over the pasta with grated Parmesan.

# Spelt pasta with Mediterranean vegetables

SERVES: 4 | PREP TIME: 10 MINUTES | COOKING TIME: 30 MINUTES

### INGREDIENTS

500 g / 1 lb 2 oz / 2 cups spelt pasta shapes

2 tbsp olive oil

1 red onion, peeled and finely chopped

1 clove garlic, chopped

1 aubergine (eggplant), finely chopped

285 g / 10 oz / jar artichoke hearts, drained and halved

1 handful thyme leaves

250 ml / 9 fl. oz / 1 cup double (heavy) cream

2 tbsp Parmesan, grated, to serve

### METHOD

1. Cook the pasta in boiling water according to the packet instructions. Drain and toss with a little oil then keep warm.

2. Meanwhile heat the oil in a pan and fry the red onion very gently for about 15 minutes until very sweet and tender.

3. Add the garlic and aubergine and cook for about 10 minutes, seasoning lightly, until the aubergine is cooked.

4. Stir in the artichokes, thyme and cream and adjust the seasoning. Toss the pasta with the sauce and serve with grated Parmesan.

# Tortellini in tomato sauce

SERVES: 2 | PREP TIME: 5 MINUTES | COOKING TIME: 15 MINUTES

## INGREDIENTS

2 tbsp olive oil

1 onion, finely chopped

1 clove garlic, finely chopped

400 g / 14 oz / 2 cups chopped tomatoes

1 handful thyme leaves

500 g / 1 lb 2 oz / 2 cups ready-made fresh tortellini, such as spinach and ricotta

## METHOD

1. Heat the oil in a pan and sweat the onion and garlic without colouring.

2. Add the tomatoes and a splash of water and simmer for 10 minutes, then stir in the thyme leaves and season.

3. Cook the pasta in boiling water according to the packet instructions then drain well.

4. Toss the pasta with the sauce and serve.

# Noodle soup

SERVES: 4 | PREP TIME: 10 MINUTES | COOKING TIME: 15-20 MINUTES

## INGREDIENTS

1 tbsp olive oil

1 onion, peeled and finely chopped

1 celery stalk, finely chopped

1 carrot, peeled and finely chopped

1 clove of garlic, finely chopped

1 L / 2 pints / 5 cups vegetable stock

80 g / 3 oz / ¼ cup spaghetti

1 nutmeg

salt and pepper

2 tbsp Parmesan cheese, grated

extra virgin olive oil

## METHOD

1. Heat the olive oil in a pan.

2. Add the onion, celery and carrot and sweat until softened.

3. Add the garlic and cook for a further minute Pour in the stock and bring to a simmer

4. Break the pasta into lots of small pieces. Add the pasta and cook until 'al dente' or until just tender.

5. Grate over a little nutmeg and adjust the seasoning. Serve with Parmesan cheese and oil for drizzling.

# Linguine with peas and watercress

SERVES: 4 | PREP TIME: 5 MINUTES | COOKING TIME: 15 MINUTES

## INGREDIENTS

500 g / 1 lb / 2 cups linguine

150 g / 5 oz / ⅔ cup peas

1 pack watercress, chopped

4 tbsp butter

½ lemon, juiced

4 tbsp Parmesan, grated

## METHOD

1. Cook the linguine in boiling salted water according to the packet instructions.

2. 4 minutes from the end of cooking time add the peas. When cooked, drain, reserving a little of the cooking water.

3. Melt the butter in a pan and wilt the watercress a little. Toss in the pasta and peas with 1-2 tablespoons of cooking water and season with salt and pepper.

4. Squeeze over a little lemon juice and serve with Parmesan.

# Greens and pasta salad

SERVES: 4 | PREP TIME: 20 MINUTES | COOKING TIME: 15 MINUTES

## INGREDIENTS

400g / 14 oz / 3 ½ cups orecchiette pasta
1 courgette (zucchini)
1 fennel bulb, root trimmed
2 celery stalks, finely chopped
1 tbsp mint, chopped
1 tbsp basil, chopped
110 ml / 4 fl. oz / ½ cup olive oil
1 lemon, juiced
ground mixed peppercorns

## METHOD

1. Cook the pasta in boiling water according to the packet instructions. Drain and toss with olive oil.

2. Meanwhile, cut the courgette into small matchsticks and squeeze over a little lemon juice and salt to macerate.

3. Finely chop the fennel and add to the courgette, along with the celery and herbs and mix well.

4. Once the pasta is cooked, toss with the vegetables and add more oil to lubricate.

5. Season well with the ground mixed peppercorns then serve.

# Pasta alla norma

SERVES: 2 | PREP TIME: 10 MINUTES | COOKING TIME: 30 MINUTES

## INGREDIENTS

1 aubergine (eggplant), sliced

a pinch of sea salt

50 ml / 1 ¾ fl. oz / ¼ cup olive oil

1 onion, diced

1 clove of garlic, thinly sliced

a pinch of chilli (chili) flakes

a handful of fresh basil, roughly chopped

400 g / 14 oz canned chopped tomatoes

120 g / 4 ¼ oz penne pasta

1 tbsp plain (all-purpose) flour

50 g / 1 ¾ oz / ½ cup Pecorino cheese, grated

## METHOD

1. Place the sliced aubergine into a colander over the sink. Sprinkle over the salt to draw out moisture.

2. Heat 1 tablespoon of the olive oil in a pan over a medium heat. Add the onion and cook for 5 minutes. Add the garlic and chilli flakes and cook for 1 more minute. Add most of the basil and tomatoes to the pan, cover and turn down to a simmer. Cook for 20 minutes until thickened.

3. Cook the pasta in boiling water for 15 minutes. Drain and add to the pan with the tomato sauce.

4. Heat the remaining oil in a frying pan over a mid-high heat. Lightly flour the aubergine slices and fry in the hot pan for 3 minutes until softened.

5. To serve, spoon the pasta and sauce onto a plate and top with the sliced aubergine. Sprinkle over the cheese and garnish with the remaining basil.

143

# Penne with green and black olives

SERVES: 4 | PREP TIME: 5 MINUTES | COOKING TIME: 25 MINUTES

## INGREDIENTS

500 g / 1 lb / 2 cups penne pasta

2 tbsp olive oil

1 clove garlic, finely sliced

800 g / 1 ¾ lbs / 4 cups chopped tomatoes

1 handful mixed green and black olives

4 tbsp Parmesan, to serve

a sprig of basil, to serve

## METHOD

1. Cook the pasta in boiling salted water according to the packet instructions.

2. Meanwhile heat the olive oil in a pan until quite hot, throw in the garlic and the tomatoes. Cover with a lid as it will spit.

3. When the spitting dies down, remove the lid and stir in the olives. Season and remove from the heat.

4. Drain the pasta and toss with the sauce.

5. Serve with grated Parmesan and a sprig of basil.

144

# Ravioli with mushrooms

SERVES: 2 | PREP TIME: 5 MINUTES | COOKING TIME: 20 MINUTES

## INGREDIENTS

2 tbsp olive oil

200g / 6 ½ oz / ¾ cup mushrooms, chopped

2 sprigs thyme

1 clove garlic, chopped

400g / 14 oz / 2 cups chopped tomatoes

500g / 1lb / 2 cups ready-made fresh ravioli,
such as wild mushroom

2 tbsp Parmesan, grated to serve

## METHOD

1. Heat the oil in a pan and add the mushrooms
with the thyme and garlic.

2. Cook briskly until the liquid evaporates,
season then add the tomatoes and
a splash of water.

3. Simmer for 10 minutes.

4. Meanwhile, cook the pasta in boiling salted
water according to the packet instructions.

5. Drain then toss with the sauce.

6. Serve with Parmesan.

# Garlic and parsley spaghetti

SERVES: 4 | PREP TIME: 2 MINUTES | COOKING TIME: 12 MINUTES

## INGREDIENTS

400 g / 14 oz spaghetti

100 ml / 3 ½ fl. oz / ½ cup olive oil

2 tsp red pepper flakes

125 g / 4 ½ oz / 1 ½ cups sourdough or ciabatta breadcrumbs

4 cloves of garlic, finely chopped

2 tbsp flat-leaved parsley, finely chopped

## METHOD

1. Boil the pasta in salted water according to the packet instructions.

2. Meanwhile, heat the oil in a large sauté pan and fry the pepper flakes and breadcrumbs until they turn golden.

3. Add the garlic and parsley and continue to stir-fry until the breadcrumbs are crisp.

4. Reserve a cup of the pasta cooking water and drain the rest. Add two thirds of the breadcrumb mixture and toss to coat, adding a little of the cooking water if it looks too dry.

5. Divide between four warm bowls and top with the rest of the breadcrumb mixture.

# Tagliatelle with vegetables and cream

SERVES: 4 | PREP TIME: 10 MINUTES | COOKING TIME: 10 MINUTES

## INGREDIENTS

500g / 1 lb / 2 cups tagliatelle
1 tbsp butter
1 shallot, finely chopped
1 clove of garlic, finely chopped
1 courgette, diced
1 red pepper, deseeded and diced
00ml / 13 ½ fl oz / 1 ½ cups double (heavy) cream or crème fraiche
salt and pepper
3 tbsp Parmesan, grated

## METHOD

1. Heat the butter in a pan and sweat the shallot and garlic without colouring.

2. Once softened, add the diced courgette and pepper and cook until tender.

3. Cook the pasta according to the packet instructions. Drain and toss with a little oil.

4. Add the cream to the vegetables and season well. Toss the pasta with the cream sauce and serve with Parmesan and a good grind of black pepper.

# Spinach cannelloni with tomato and basil sauce

SERVES: 4 | PREP TIME: 40 MINUTES | COOKING TIME: 25 MINUTES

## INGREDIENTS

12 cannelloni tubes or 12 sheets lasagne

handful Cheddar, grated

### FOR THE FILLING:

2 tbsp butter

olive oil

2 cloves garlic, chopped

nutmeg, grated

1 kg / 2 lb 4 oz spinach leaves, wilted

400 g / 14 oz ricotta

2 tbsp Parmesan, grated

### FOR THE TOMATO SAUCE:

2 tbsp olive oil

1 clove garlic, chopped

400 g / 14 oz / 2 cups chopped tomatoes

200 ml / 7 fl. oz / 1 cup water

1 tbsp basil, chopped

## METHOD

1. Preheat the oven to 180°C (160° fan) / 350F / gas 5.

2. Heat the butter in a pan with oil and cook the garlic for 2 minutes. Add the spinach and nutmeg and stir until the spinach is wilted.

3. Spoon into a sieve and press down firmly with a wooden spoon to extract as much liquid as possible. Once done, finely chop the spinach and leave to cool in a bowl.

4. Stir in the ricotta, Parmesan and seasoning then mix well.

5. Spoon into the tubes or onto the lasagne sheets and roll up to make 12 cylinders.

6. Place 2-3 of the tubes in each greased dish.

7. To make the tomato sauce, heat the oil in a pan and add the garlic and tomatoes. Leave to simmer, topped up with water, for 10 minutes, then add the basil and season with salt and pepper.

8. Spoon the tomato sauce over the cannelloni in each dish, then sprinkle the Cheddar over the sauce and bake for around 15 minutes until bubbling.

# Faggottini with basil

SERVES: 4 | PREP TIME: 25 MINUTES | COOKING TIME: 2 MINUTES

## INGREDIENTS

500 g / 1 lb recipe pasta rolled into 2 sheets

FOR THE FILLING:

1 large bunch basil, chopped

200 g / 6 ½ oz / ¾ cup ricotta

1 tbsp olive oil

60 g / 2 oz / ⅓ cup butter

several basil sprigs

½ lemon, grated zest

## METHOD

1. Stir the chopped basil into the ricotta with oil.

2. Lay a sheet of pasta onto a floured work surface and place teaspoonfuls of the mixture at intervals along the sheet, leaving a 5 cm (2 in) gap between each mound. Brush around each mound with a little beaten egg or water.

3. Top with the second sheet of pasta. Press down lightly around each mound. Cut out each piece with a knife and lay them on a baking tray.

4. Cover the ravioli with a damp tea towel until ready to cook.

5. Cook the ravioli in boiling water for 2 minutes. Remove with a slotted spoon and drain on kitchen paper.

6. Toss gently with the melted butter and top with basil leaves and lemon zest.

# Pappardelle with tomato sauce

SERVES: 4 | PREP TIME: 5 MINUTES | COOKING TIME: 15 MINUTES

## INGREDIENTS

500 g / 1 lb / 2 cups pappardelle pasta

FOR THE SAUCE:

2 tbsp olive oil

1 onion, finely chopped

1 clove garlic, finely chopped

400 g / 14 oz / 2 cups chopped tomatoes

1 handful thyme leaves

3 tbsp ricotta

## METHOD

1. Heat the oil in a pan and sweat the onion and garlic without colouring.

2. Add the tomatoes with a splash of water and the thyme and leave to simmer for 10 minutes.

3. Cook the pasta in boiling salted water for 10 minutes or according to the packet instructions, then drain.

4. Stir the ricotta into the tomato sauce then toss the pasta in the sauce.

5. Season with salt and pepper and serve.

# Green pesto pasta salad

SERVES: 4-6 | PREP TIME: 5 MINUTES | COOKING TIME: 12 MINUTES

## INGREDIENTS

500 g / 1 lb / 2 cups farfalle pasta
1 tbsp olive oil
6 tbsp green pesto
salt and pepper
2 tbsp Parmesan, grated

## METHOD

1. Cook the pasta in boiling, salted water according to the packet instructions or until al dente.

2. Toss the pasta with the pesto and the olive oil and season to taste.

3. Serve sprinkled with Parmesan.

# Farfalle with spicy cherry tomatoes

SERVES: 4 | PREP TIME: 5 MINUTES | COOKING TIME: 12 MINUTES

### INGREDIENTS

500 g / 1 lb / 2 cups farfalle pasta

2 tbsp olive oil

2 cloves garlic, finely chopped

1 tbsp sage leaves, chopped

300 g / 10 oz / 1 ¼ cups cherry tomatoes, halved

Tabasco, to taste

### METHOD

1. Cook the pasta as per the packet instructions.

2. Heat the olive oil in a pan. Add the garlic and sage leaves. Fry the sage leaves until crisp, then remove from the pan and drain on kitchen paper.

3. Add the tomatoes and toss in the flavoured oil until just tender, then sprinkle with Tabasco to taste. Season and remove from the heat.

4. Drain the pasta – not too thoroughly – then toss with the tomatoes and sage leaves.

5. Serve with more Tabasco if desired.

# Maltagliata with artichokes

SERVES: 4 | PREP TIME: 15 MINUTES | COOKING TIME: 35 MINUTES

## INGREDIENTS

12 lasagne sheets

4 globe artichokes, prepared in acidulated water

1 handful black olives

1 handful green olives

½ medium courgette, halved and thinly sliced

2 confit lemons, quartered

2 tbsp olive oil

salt and pepper

## METHOD

1. Using a non-iron or aluminium pan, boil the artichokes in salted, acidulated water for about 30 minutes, or until one of the outer leaves pulls away easily. Drain and cut into quarters.

2. Cut the lasagne sheets into irregular shapes (maltagliata means malformed in Italian).

3. Cook in boiling water according to the packet instructions then drain.

4. Heat the oil in a pan with the confit lemons and gently warm the artichokes, olives and courgette slices through in the oil. Season well.

5. Toss with the pasta shapes and serve.

# Penne with chilli tomato sauce

SERVES: 4 | PREP TIME: 5 MINUTES | COOKING TIME: 12 MINUTES

### INGREDIENTS

500 g / 1lb / 2 cups penne pasta
2 tbsp olive oil
2 cloves garlic, chopped
1 red chilli (chili), chopped
400 g / 14 oz / 2 cups chopped tomatoes
a pinch of micro basil leaves

### METHOD

1. Cook the pasta according to the packet instructions in boiling salted water.

2. Meanwhile heat the oil in a pan and gently fry the garlic and chilli.

3. Add the tomatoes, turn the heat up and bubble briskly for 10 minutes.

4. Drain the pasta and toss with the sauce then stir in the basil. Serve hot.

# Tagliatelle with leeks

SERVES: 4 | PREP TIME: 10 MINUTES | COOKING TIME: 20 MINUTES

## INGREDIENTS

500g / 1 lb / 2 cups tagliatelle

3 tbsp butter

2 leeks, trimmed and finely sliced

2 sprigs thyme

300 ml / 10 fl. oz / 1 ¼ cups passata

salt and pepper

## METHOD

1. Cook the pasta in boiling salted water according to the packet instructions.

2. Drain and toss with a little oil.

3. Meanwhile, heat the butter in a pan and add the leeks and thyme with a little salt. Cook very gently until soft and sweet.

4. Add the passata and leave to simmer for 10 minutes.

5. Adjust the seasoning in the sauce, adding salt and pepper to taste.

6. Drain the pasta and toss with the sauce before serving or place the pasta in the bowls then spoon the sauce on top.

# Spiral pasta with tomato and basil

SERVES: 4 | PREP TIME: 5 MINUTES | COOKING TIME: 12 MINUTES

## INGREDIENTS

500 g / 1 lb / 2 cups spirali pasta
2 tbsp olive oil
1 clove garlic, finely sliced
800 g / 1 ¾ lbs / 4 cups chopped tomatoes
2 tbsp basil, roughly chopped
1 ball mozzarella

## METHOD

1. Cook the pasta in boiling salted water according to the packet instructions.

2. Meanwhile heat the olive oil in a pan until quite hot, throw in the garlic and the tomatoes. Cover with a lid as it will spit.

3. When the spitting dies down, remove the lid and stir in the basil, season and remove from the heat.

4. Drain the pasta and toss with the sauce.

5. Stir in chunks of mozzarella and serve.

# Tomato and purple basil spaghetti

SERVES: 4 | PREP TIME: 2 MINUTES | COOKING TIME: 12 MINUTES

## INGREDIENTS

400 g / 14 oz spaghetti

100 ml / 3 ½ fl. oz / ½ cup olive oil

2 cloves of garlic, unpeeled and squashed

1 small bunch thyme, leaves only

200 g / 7 oz / 1 ½ cups cherry tomatoes, halved

1 large handful purple basil leaves

## METHOD

1. Boil the pasta in salted water according to the packet instructions or until al dente.

2. Meanwhile, heat the oil in a large sauté pan with the garlic. When it starts to sizzle, discard the garlic.

3. Stir in the thyme leaves and cook over a low heat for 1 minute. Add the cherry tomatoes and let them warm through.

4. Drain the pasta, then toss with the tomatoes and thyme in the sauté pan. Divide between four warm bowls and garnish with purple basil.

# Romanesco cauliflower lasagne

SERVES: 4-6 | PREP TIME: 30 MINUTES | COOKING TIME: 40 MINUTES

## INGREDIENTS

500 g / 1 lb 2 oz / 2 cups broccoli,
separated into florets

500 g / 1 lb 2 oz / 2 cups romanesco cauliflower,
separated into florets

3 tbsp olive oil

4 cloves garlic, finely chopped

1 tbsp thyme

6 anchovies, chopped

1 pinch dried chilli (chili) flakes

12 lasagne sheets

500 ml / 18 fl. oz / 2 cups ricotta

200 g / 7 oz / ¾ cup Parmesan, grated

200 g / 7 oz / ¾ cup mozzarella cheese

## METHOD

1. Preheat the oven to 190°C (170°) / 375F / gas 5.

2. Boil the cauliflower and broccoli for 5 minutes then drain, reserving the cooking water.

3. Heat 1 tablespoon of oil in a pan and add the garlic, thyme, anchovies and chilli flakes. Allow the anchovies to melt, then stir in the florets and 5 tablespoons of cooking water.

4. Cover partially with a lid and cook for 20 minutes until the vegetables are tender. Lightly crush and season, then leave to cool.

5. Lay 4 of the lasagne sheets in a buttered baking dish.

6. Stir the ricotta and half the Parmesan into the cooled vegetables then spread half over the pasta. Top with 4 sheets of pasta, repeat and finish with a layer of pasta.

7. Place the sliced mozzarella and Parmesan over the top, drizzle with oil and bake for about 30 minutes, until bubbling and golden.

8. Serve hot or warm.

# Wild mushroom and shallot cannelloni

SERVES: 6 | PREP TIME: 25 MINUTES | COOKING TIME: 30 MINUTES

## INGREDIENTS

3 tbsp olive oil

2 shallots, finely chopped

1 onion, finely chopped

1 clove garlic, finely chopped

500 g / 1 lb 2 oz / 2 cups wild mushrooms

18 cannelloni tubes

4 tbsp parsley, chopped

100 ml / 3 ½ fl. oz / ½ cup double (heavy) cream

40 g butter

3 tbsp Parmesan, grated

## METHOD

1. Preheat the oven to 200°C / 400F / gas 6.

2. Heat the oil in a casserole pan and add the shallot and onion. Cook for a few minutes, stirring regularly.

3. Add the mushrooms and garlic and cook until the liquid has evaporated. Season with salt and pepper, then add the parsley and cream.

4. Reduce until the cream has almost gone, then remove from the heat.

5. Cook the cannelloni tubes in boiling salted water according to the packet instructions. Drain thoroughly and pat dry.

6. Stuff the cannelloni tubes with the mushroom mixture – either use a piping bag or a teaspoon.

7. Place in a buttered baking dish and sprinkle with Parmesan and a few dots of butter.

8. Cook in the oven for 10 minutes then serve.

# Penne with orange and mushrooms

SERVES: 4 | PREP TIME: 10 MINUTES | COOKING TIME: 15 MINUTES

## INGREDIENTS

500 g / 1 lb 2 oz / 2 cups penne pasta

2 tbsp butter

olive oil

2 handfuls mixed wild mushrooms, torn

1 small orange, segmented

1 handful sage leaves, chopped

salt and pepper

4 tbsp Parmesan, grated

## METHOD

1. Cook the pasta in boiling salted water according to the packet instructions.

2. Drain, reserving a little of the water. Toss with olive oil.

3. Meanwhile, heat the butter in a pan and cook the mushrooms until the liquid has evaporated.

4. Add the orange segments and sage leaves and season.

5. Toss the pasta with the mushrooms and 2 tablespoons of cooking water.

6. Serve scattered generously with grated Parmesan.

# Raviolone with artichokes

SERVES: 4 | PREP TIME: 1 HOUR | COOKING TIME: 10 MINUTES

## INGREDIENTS

500 g / 1 lb 2 oz /pasta dough, chilled

FOR THE FILLING:
400 g / 14 oz / 1 ½ cups Jerusalem artichokes
80 g / 3 oz / ⅓ cup butter
2 tbsp cream
12 quail eggs

FOR THE SAUCE:
4 tbsp butter
2 tsp black truffle juice
2 tomatoes, peeled, seeded and finely chopped
½ bunch chives, finely chopped

## METHOD

1. Boil the artichokes in water for 10 minutes. Drain then tip into a liquidizer with the butter and cream. Blend to a puree. Leave to cool.

2. Remove the pasta from the fridge. Using a pasta machine, roll out the dough into sheets about 1-2mm thick and 10 cm (4 in) wide.

3. Place 1 teaspoon of filling in the middle of the sheet at one end. Create a well in the centre and crack an egg into it. Repeat all the way along at 5 cm (2 in) intervals. Brush water around each filling. Place a sheet of pasta on top, then, working from one end to the other, push the sheets together around each mound of filling. Cut out each ravioli shape.

4. Cook the ravioli in boiling water for 1 minute. Heat the butter in a pan with 2 teaspoons of truffle juice. Pour over the ravioli. Decorate with chives.

168

# Grilled ravioli
# with asparagus

SERVES: 2 | PREP TIME: 10 MINUTES | COOKING TIME: 5 MINUTES

## INGREDIENTS

500 g / 1lb 2 oz / 2 cups ready-made fresh ravioli,
spinach and ricotta

8 stalks asparagus, woody ends snapped off

200 g / 7 oz / ¾ cup Fontina cheese

## METHOD

1. Cook the pasta in boiling water according
   to the packet instructions, then drain and
   toss with a little butter.

2. Cut the asparagus into short lengths
   and parboil in salted water for 3 minutes.
   Drain and pat dry.

3. Tip the ravioli and asparagus into a greased
   baking dish, season lightly and cover with
   slices of fontina.

4. Grill until bubbling.

169

# Penne all'arrabiata

SERVES: 4 | PREP TIME: 5 MINUTES | COOKING TIME: 12 MINUTES

### INGREDIENTS

500 g / 1 lb 2 oz / 2 cups penne pasta
2 tbsp olive oil
2 cloves garlic, chopped
1 red chilli (chili), chopped
400 g / 14 oz / 2 cups chopped tomatoes
1 tbsp basil, chopped

### METHOD

1. Cook the pasta according to the packet instructions in boiling salted water.

2. Meanwhile, heat the oil in a pan and gently fry the garlic and chilli.

3. Add the tomatoes, turn the heat up and bubble briskly for 10 minutes.

4. Drain the pasta and toss with the sauce then stir in the basil.

5. Serve hot.

# Spaghetti with broccoli

SERVES: 2 | PREP TIME: 10 MINUTES | COOKING TIME: 15 MINUTES

## INGREDIENTS

300 g / 10 ½ oz head of broccoli

120 g / 4 ¼ oz spaghetti

1 tbsp olive oil

1 clove of garlic, minced

1 lemon, juice and zest

125 ml / 4 ½ fl. oz / ½ cup white wine

150 ml / 5 ¼ fl. oz / ⅔ cup double (heavy) cream

a handful of flat-leaved parsley, chopped

25 g / 1 oz Parmesan cheese, grated

## METHOD

1. Cut the florets from the head of broccoli, place into a pan of boiling salted water and cook for 8-10 minutes. Drain and set aside.

2. Place the pasta into a pan of salted boiling water and cook for 12-15 minutes until tender. Drain and set aside.

3. Heat the oil in a pan on a medium heat. Fry the garlic for 1 minute. Add the lemon and wine to the pan. Cook for 2-3 minutes.

4. Add the cream to the pan followed by the broccoli, pasta and parsley. Toss to coat and heat the pasta and vegetables through.

5. Add to serving bowls and top with cheese.

# Minestrone vegetable soup

SERVES: 4 | PREP TIME: 20 MINUTES | COOKING TIME: 45 MINUTES

## INGREDIENTS

2 tbsp olive oil

1 onion, diced

2 celery stick, chopped

2 carrots, sliced

2 cloves of garlic, chopped

400 g / 14 oz canned chopped tomatoes

1 litre chicken or vegetable stock

240 g / 8 ½ oz red kidney beans, drained

150 g / 5 ¼ oz spaghetti, broken into smaller pieces

200 g / 7 oz / 1 ⅓ cups garden peas, frozen

a handful flat-leaved parsley leaves

sea salt and freshly ground black pepper

## METHOD

1. Heat the oil in a saucepan with a lid over a medium heat. Add the onion, celery and carrot. Cook for 8-10 minutes. Add the garlic. Cook for a further minute.

2. Add the chopped tomatoes followed by the chicken stock. Bring to the boil before placing the lid on top. Reduce the heat to a simmer. Cook for 10-15 minutes.

3. Add the beans and pasta to the pan and cook for a further 12-15 minutes until the pasta is cooked. Add the peas for the last 3-5 minutes to cook. Check the seasoning to taste and add more water if the soup is too thick.

4. To serve, ladle the soup into bowls and top with the parsley.

172

# Spaghetti with herbs and chanterelle

SERVES: 2 | PREP TIME: 10 MINUTES | COOKING TIME: 20 MINUTES

## INGREDIENTS

120 g / 4 ¼ oz spaghetti

1 tbsp olive oil

20 g / ¾ oz butter

1 clove of garlic, minced

150 g / 5 ¼ oz chanterelle mushrooms

a handful of parsley, chopped

a few sprigs of fresh thyme

50 g / 1 ¾ oz / ½ cup Parmesan shards

## METHOD

1. Cook the spaghetti as per the packet instructions, drain and set aside.

2. Heat the oil and butter in a pan over a mid-high heat. Once the butter is frothy, add the garlic. Fry for 1 minute then add the mushrooms and herbs. Fry in the butter and garlic for 3 minutes, moving them around the pan at all time.

3. Add the spaghetti to the pan and toss to coat with the juices from the pan.

4. Place onto serving plates with the shards of Parmesan cheese.

# Cherry tomatoes with spaghetti

SERVES: 2 | PREP TIME: 10 MINUTES | COOKING TIME: 20 MINUTES

## INGREDIENTS

2 tbsp olive oil

1 onion, diced

2 cloves of garlic, minced

175 ml / 6 fl. oz / ⅔ cup red wine

250 g / 9 oz cherry tomatoes

120 g / 4 ¼ oz spaghetti

1 handful basil, chopped

sea salt and black pepper

extra virgin olive oil, to drizzle

## METHOD

1. Preheat the oven to 180°C (160°C fan) / 350F / gas 4.

2. Heat half the olive oil in a pan over a medium heat. Cook the onions and garlic for 4-5 minutes.

3. Turn up the heat. Add the wine to the pan. Let the liquid bubble until reduced in volume by half. Chop half the tomatoes and add to the pan, turn down the heat to a simmer and cover.

4. Pour the remaining oil over the rest of the tomatoes. Place in the oven to roast for 6 minutes. Add the roast tomatoes to the tomato sauce.

5. Cook the pasta as per the packet instructions. Drain and add the pasta to plates. Add the roast tomatoes in sauce. Scatter with chopped basil and drizzle with extra virgin olive oil.

# Feta and beetroot penne

SERVES: 2 | PREP TIME: 10 MINUTES | COOKING TIME: 1 HOUR

## INGREDIENTS

2 medium-sized beetroots

2 cloves of garlic

a few sprigs of thyme

2 tbsp olive oil

150 ml / 5 ¼ fl. oz / ⅔ cup vegetable stock

150 g / 5 ¼ oz penne pasta

100 g / 3 ½ oz feta cheese, crumbled

a small bunch of basil, chopped

sea salt and cracked black pepper

## METHOD

1. Preheat the oven to 180°C (160°C fan) / 350F / gas 4.

2. Peel and dice the beetroot and add to a baking tray with the garlic, thyme and oil. Toss to coat everything in the oil and roast in the oven for around 45 minutes until the beetroot is tender.

3. Remove from the oven and discard the thyme. Add the beetroot to the cup of a blender and squeeze the garlic out of its skins into the blender. Blend to a puree. Add enough of the stock to make this more of a sauce consistency. Add to a saucepan and gently heat through.

4. Cook the pasta as per the packet instructions. Drain and add the pasta to the beetroot sauce, stir to coat and mix through and season with salt and black pepper.

5. Add to warmed serving plates and scatter with the crumbled feta cheese and basil.

# Mushroom and spinach spaghetti

SERVES: 2 | PREP TIME: 10 MINUTES | COOKING TIME: 15 MINUTES

## INGREDIENTS

150 g / 5 ¼ oz spaghetti

2 tsp olive oil

100 g / 3 ½ oz mushrooms, sliced

150 g / 5 ¼ oz spinach, washed

1 tsp nutmeg, grated

sea salt and cracked black pepper

## METHOD

1. Cook the spaghetti as per the packet instructions.

2. Heat half the oil in a frying pan over a medium high heat and add the mushrooms. Fry for 5-8 minutes until the mushrooms start to release their moisture.

3. Add the spinach to the mushrooms and stir through the mushrooms. As the spinach releases its liquid, pour it from the pan. Once wilted, add the nutmeg and season with salt and black pepper.

4. Add the cooked spaghetti to the pan with the mushrooms and spinach and mix through to coat the pasta.

# Radiatore with vegetables

SERVES: 2 | PREP TIME: 15 MINUTES | COOKING TIME: 30 MINUTES

## INGREDIENTS

1 tbsp olive oil

1 red onion, diced

2 carrots, diced

2 cloves garlic, minced

1 tbsp tomato puree

150 ml / 5 ¼ fl. oz / ⅔ cup vegetable stock

100 g / 3 ½ oz / ½ cup sundried tomatoes

200 g / 7 oz flageolet beans

200 g / 7 oz wholewheat radiatori pasta

## METHOD

1. Heat the oil in a large heavy bottomed pan. Add the onion and fry for 3-5 minutes then add the carrots. Cook for a further 2-3 minutes then add the garlic and cook for a further minute.

2. Add the tomato puree. Stir through the vegetables. Add the vegetable stock. Adjust the heat to a simmer, cover and cook for 20 minutes. Add the tomatoes and beans after 10 minutes.

3. Cook the pasta as per the packet instructions. Drain and add to the pan with the vegetables.

4. Season and mix the pasta through the vegetables to coat with the flavours.

# Tagliatelle with pesto

SERVES: 2 | PREP TIME: 15 MINUTES | COOKING TIME: 15 MINUTES

## INGREDIENTS

a large bunch of basil, chopped

a large bunch of parsley, chopped

1 clove of garlic

50 ml / 1 ¾ fl. oz / ¼ cup extra virgin olive oil

1 lemon, zest and juice

25 g Parmesan cheese, grated

150 g / 5 ¼ oz tagliatelle

25 g pine nuts, toasted

2 sprigs basil, to serve

## METHOD

1. Place the first six ingredients into a blender and blend for 1 minute until combined. If a little thick, add some more oil. Season with salt and black pepper.

2. Place the pasta into a pan of boiling salted water as per the packet instructions then drain and return to the pan.

3. Add the pesto to the pan with the pasta and mix to thoroughly coat.

4. Spoon into warmed serving bowls and garnish with the toasted pine nuts and a sprig of basil.

179

Perfect Pasta

# Cheese dishes

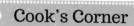

# Parmesan pumpkin pasta bake

SERVES: 4 | PREP TIME: 20 MINUTES | COOKING TIME: 55 MINUTES

## INGREDIENTS

1 small butternut squash, peeled and cubed

2 tbsp olive oil

1 tbsp fresh thyme leaves

600 ml / 1 pint / 2 ½ cups milk

400 g / 14 oz / 4 cups dried macaroni

2 tbsp butter

1 ½ tbsp plain flour

150 g / 5 ½ oz / 1 ½ cups Parmesan cheese, grated

150 g / 5 ½ oz / 1 ½ cups Cheddar cheese, grated

## METHOD

1. Preheat the oven to 190°C (170°C fan) / 375F / gas 5.

2. Toss the squash with the oil and thyme and season with salt and pepper. Spread it out in a large roasting tin and roast for 30 minutes, turning halfway through.

3. Transfer the squash to a liquidizer and blend with the milk until smooth.

4. Cook the macaroni in boiling, salted water for 10 minutes or until almost cooked. Drain well.

5. Meanwhile, pour the squash milk into a saucepan and add the butter and flour. Stir over a medium heat until it thickens and starts to simmer.

6. Take the pan off the heat and stir in the cheese for 2-3 minutes until melted. Stir in the macaroni then scrape into a baking dish.

7. Bake for 45 minutes or until the top is golden brown and the pasta is cooked.

# Feta and artichoke cannelloni

SERVES: 6 | PREP TIME: 30 MINUTES | COOKING TIME: 1 HOUR 30 MINUTES

## INGREDIENTS

6 globe artichokes

1 lemon, juiced

4 tbsp olive oil

1 onion, peeled and chopped

2 cloves garlic, chopped

200 ml / 7 fl. oz white wine

12 sheets of lasagne pasta

200 g / 7 oz / 1 ⅓ cups feta

400 ml / 14 fl. oz / 2 cups passata

2 tbsp basil, chopped

## METHOD

1. Remove some of the tough outer leaves of the artichokes, snap off the stalk and snap away the stem.

2. Spread the leaves apart and dig out the central cone with a teaspoon. Scrape out the choke underneath.

3. Place the artichokes in acidulated water. Heat the oil in a casserole pan and add the artichokes, onion, garlic and white wine and cook for 1 hour.

4. Meanwhile, preheat the oven to 180°C (160° fan) / 350F / gas 4. Cook the lasagne sheets according to the packet instructions. Drain and lay out on a work surface.

5. Chop the basil and feta, setting a little aside for the sauce. Spoon the artichoke mixture and feta and basil down one half of each sheet then roll up to form a cylinder.

6. Place in a roasting tin and cover with tomato sauce and sprinkle with reserved feta and basil.

7. Bake for 15 minutes and serve warm.

# Pasta with mussels in Gorgonzola sauce

SERVES: 4 | PREP TIME: 15 MINUTES | COOKING TIME: 12 MINUTES

## INGREDIENTS

500 g / 1 lb 2 oz / 4 ½ cups farfalle pasta

1 tbsp butter

1 shallot, finely chopped

1 red pepper, deseeded and finely chopped

1 clove garlic, chopped

500 g / 1 lb 2 oz / 3 ⅓ cups mussels, cleaned

100 ml / 3 ½ fl. oz / ½ cup pastis

120 g / 4 ½ oz / ½ cup Gorgonzola

120 g / 4 ½ oz / ½ cup mascarpone

## METHOD

1. Cook the pasta as per the packet instructions. Once cooked, drain, toss with a little oil and keep warm.

2. Meanwhile, heat the butter in a pan and add the shallot, pepper and garlic.

3. Once softened add the mussels and pastis, allow to bubble up then cover with a lid and leave to simmer for about 5 minutes or until the mussels have opened.

4. Carefully tip the mussels into a colander over a large bowl to collect the cooking liquor, leaving any sediment behind in the bottom and discarding any mussels that remain closed.

5. Heat the Gorgonzola and mascarpone in a pan then add a little of the reserved cooking liquor and season with black pepper.

6. Remove the meat from most of the mussels and add to the pan with the pasta.

7. Serve decorated with remaining mussel shells.

# Macaroni cheese

SERVES: 4 | PREP TIME: 20 MINUTES | COOKING TIME: 30 MINUTES

● ● ● ● ● ● ● ● ● ● ● ● ● ● ● ● ● ● ● ● ● ● ● ● ● ●

## INGREDIENTS

250 g / 9 oz / 1 cup macaroni pasta

40 g butter

40 g flour

600 ml / 1 pint 2 fl. oz / 2 ½ cups milk

250 g / 9 oz / 1 cup Gruyère, grated

4 tbsp Parmesan, grated

4 slices good-quality ham, finely chopped

nutmeg, grated

## METHOD

1.  Preheat the oven to 180°C / 350F / gas 4.

2.  Cook the pasta in boiling water according to the packet instructions. Drain and toss with a little oil to prevent sticking.

3.  Meanwhile, heat the butter in a pan and, once foaming, add the flour. Stir to form a paste, then whisk in the milk a little at a time.

4.  Add all the milk, whisking to ensure the sauce is smooth, then reduce the heat and cook for 10 minutes, whisking occasionally.

5.  Stir in the Gruyère, half the Parmesan, the ham and season with salt and pepper. Grate in a little nutmeg.

6.  Stir the macaroni into the sauce then tip into a baking dish.

7.  Scatter the Parmesan over the top and bake for 20-30 minutes until bubbling.

# Ricotta spinach cannelloni

SERVES: 4 | PREP TIME: 40 MINUTES | COOKING TIME: 30 MINUTES

## INGREDIENTS

2 tbsp butter

1 tbsp olive oil

2 cloves garlic, chopped

nutmeg, grated to taste

1 kg / 2 lbs / 4 ½ cups spinach leaves

400 g / 13 ½ oz / 1 ½ cups ricotta

2 tbsp Parmesan, grated

12 cannelloni tubes

### FOR THE TOMATO SAUCE:

2 tbsp olive oil

1 clove of garlic, chopped

2 x 400 g can chopped tomatoes

½ bunch basil, chopped

## METHOD

1. Preheat the oven to 180C / 350F / gas 5. To make the filling, heat the butter in a large pan with the oil and cook the garlic for 2 minutes.

2. Add the spinach and nutmeg and stir and toss until the spinach is completely wilted.

3. Spoon into a sieve and press down firmly with a wooden spoon to extract as much liquid as possible. Once done, finely chop the spinach and leave to cool in a bowl.

4. Stir in the ricotta, Parmesan and seasoning and mix well.

5. Spoon into the tubes or onto the lasagne sheets and roll up to make 12 cylinders, then lay in a greased baking dish.

6. To make the tomato sauce, heat the oil in a pan and add the garlic and tomatoes. Leave to simmer, topped up with half a can of water, for 10 minutes, then add the basil and season.

7. Spoon over the cannelloni and bake for around 15 minutes until bubbling.

# Penne
# with béchamel

SERVES: 4-5 | PREP TIME: 15 MINUTES | COOKING TIME: 35 MINUTES

## INGREDIENTS

500 g / 1 lb 2 oz / 2 cups penne pasta

60 g / 2 oz / ¼ cup butter

30 g / 1 oz / ⅛ cup plain (all-purpose) flour

400 ml / 14 fl. oz / 1 ¼ cups milk

nutmeg, grated

6 tbsp Parmesan, grated

## METHOD

1. Cook the pasta in boiling salted water according to the packet instructions. Drain and toss with some olive oil then keep warm.

2. Preheat the oven to 220°C (200° fan) / 425F / gas 7.

3. Heat two thirds of the butter in a pan and when foaming add the flour. Stir to make a paste and then pour in the milk a third at a time, whisking constantly to make a smooth béchamel sauce.

4. Leave to cook out for 10 minutes over a gentle heat, stirring well regularly. Season well and grate in a little nutmeg.

5. Butter a large gratin dish and tip in the pasta. Pour over the béchamel and fork through the pasta.

6. Scatter with Parmesan and a little extra butter. Place in the oven for 10-15 minutes until the top is golden and glazed.

# Macaroni with blue cheese sauce

SERVES: 4 | PREP TIME: 2 MINUTES | COOKING TIME: 12 MINUTES

## INGREDIENTS

500 g / 1 lb / 2 cups macaroni pasta

1 tbsp butter

120 g / 4 ¼ oz / ½ cup mascarpone

100 g / 3 ½ oz / ½ cup Gorgonzola, piccante
or dolce

## METHOD

1. Cook the pasta in boiling salted water according to the packet instructions.

2. Drain and toss with a little butter.

3. Meanwhile heat the mascarpone with the Gorgonzola, stirring until it melts.

4. Season generously with black pepper.

5. Toss the pasta with the sauce and serve.

# Rigatoni with pecorino

SERVES: 4 | PREP TIME: 5 MINUTES | COOKING TIME: 12 MINUTES

## INGREDIENTS

500g / 1 lb / 2 cups rigatoni pasta

60g / 2 oz / ¼ cup butter

1 clove garlic, sliced

1 handful rocket (arugula) leaves, chopped

60g / 2 oz / ¼ cup pecorino cheese, grated

## METHOD

1. Cook the pasta in boiling salted water according to the packet instructions.

2. Drain, reserving a little of the cooking water and toss in a little butter.

3. Meanwhile melt the butter in a pan with the garlic and when foaming, add the rocket.

4. Stir until the rocket is just wilted, then toss with the pasta.

5. Season and serve with the pecorino sprinkled over.

# Three-cheese orecchiette

SERVES: 4 | PREP TIME: 10 MINUTES | COOKING TIME: 15 MINUTES

## INGREDIENTS

500 g / 1 lb / 2 cups orecchiette
200 ml / 6 ½ fl. oz / ¾ cup double (heavy) cream
50 g / 2 oz / ⅓ cup Mimolette cheese, grated
50 g / 2 oz / ⅓ cup Parmesan, grated
50 g / 2 oz / ⅓ cup Gruyère or fontina, grated

## METHOD

1. Cook the orecchiette in boiling salted water according to the packet instructions.

2. Warm the cream and stir in the cheeses until they melt, reserving a little for later.

3. Season generously with black pepper and a little salt. Taste and adjust seasoning accordingly.

4. Drain the pasta and toss through the sauce.

5. Serve immediately, sprinkled with the reserved cheese.

# Orecchiette with leeks and Gorgonzola

SERVES: 4 | PREP TIME: 5 MINUTES | COOKING TIME: 15 MINUTES

## INGREDIENTS

400 g / 14 oz / 4 cups orecchiette

4 tbsp olive oil

1 large leek, trimmed and finely chopped

1 clove of garlic, crushed

50 g / 1 ¾ oz / ⅓ cup pine nuts

200 g / 7 oz / 1 cup Gorgonzola dolce

1 lemon, zest finely grated

1 handful micro leaves

## METHOD

1. Boil the pasta as per the packet instructions.

2. Meanwhile, heat 2 tablespoons of the oil in a pan. Stir-fry the leek for 8 minutes. Add the garlic. Cook for 1 minute, then take off the heat.

3. Reserve a few pine nuts for the garnish. Pound the rest with a pestle and mortar. Mash them into the fried leeks, Gorgonzola and lemon zest. Season.

4. Reserve a little pasta cooking water and drain the rest. Return the pasta to the pan. Stir in half of the Gorgonzola mixture. Add enough of the reserved cooking water to loosen.

5. Divide between four bowls. Top each one with a dollop of Gorgonzola, drizzle of oil and micro leaves.

# Deep-fried ravioli

SERVES: 6 | PREP TIME: 1 HOUR 15 MINUTES | COOKING TIME: 10 MINUTES

## INGREDIENTS

### FOR THE PASTA:
500 g / 1 lb 2 oz / 3 ⅓ cups Italian '00' flour

6 eggs

### FOR THE FILLING:
120 g / 4 oz / 1 cup Gruyère, grated

1 bunch rocket (arugula), finely chopped

40 g / 1 ½ oz / ⅓ cup Parmesan, grated

1 egg, beaten

1 bunch flat-leaved parsley, finely chopped

salt and pepper

vegetable oil, for deep frying

## METHOD

1. Place the flour in a bowl and make a well in the centre. Crack the eggs into the well.

2. Using a fork, beat the eggs and then draw in the flour a little at a time until the dough comes together. Knead the dough with your hands for 5 minutes.

3. Cover with film and chill for 30 minutes. Mix together all of the filling ingredients and stir well.

4. Using a pasta machine, roll out the dough into sheets 2 mm thick and 10 cm wide. Lay on a floured surface.

5. Place 1 tsp of filling in the middle of the sheet at one end. Repeat all the way along at 5 cm intervals and then brush a little water around each filling in a circle.

6. Place another sheet of pasta on top, then push the sheets together, around each mound of filling. Cut the ravioli into shapes using a knife or a crinkle-edged cutter.

7. Blanch the ravioli in batches in a large saucepan of salted, boiling water for 1 minute before draining well.

8. Heat the oil in a pan and cook the ravioli in batches until golden brown. Drain on kitchen paper and serve.

# Nettle and goat's cheese tortelli

SERVES: 4 | PREP TIME: 1 HOUR 15 MINUTES | COOKING TIME: 5 MINUTES

## INGREDIENTS

400 g / 14 oz / 2 ⅔ cups type '00' flour

3 medium eggs

100 g / 3 ½ oz / 4 cups stinging nettle tops,
picked with gloves

200 g / 7 oz / 1 cup fresh goat's cheese

1 lemon, zest finely grated

½ tsp freshly grated nutmeg

2 tbsp olive oil

75 g / 2 ½ oz Caprino Romano, in one piece

## METHOD

1.  Put the flour and eggs in a food processor and pulse until they form a ball of dough. Knead the dough on a lightly floured surface for 10 minutes, then wrap in clingfilm and leave to rest for 20 minutes.

2.  Meanwhile, blanch the nettles in boiling water for 1 minute, then tip into a sieve and squeeze out all the water. Transfer the nettles to a chopping board and chop finely.

3.  Mix the nettles with the goat's cheese, lemon zest and nutmeg.

4.  Roll out a quarter of the pasta dough and cut it into 10 cm circles with a cookie cutter. Add a teaspoon of the nettle mixture to the centre of each one, then fold in half to enclose. Press firmly round the edge to seal then pinch the two thin ends of the crescent together to make the classic tortelli shape.

5.  Repeat three more times to use the rest of the dough and filling.

6.  Boil the tortelli in a large pan of salted water for 4 minutes or until the pasta is cooked al dente.

7.  Divide the tortelli between four plates. Drizzle with oil then use a vegetable peeler to shave over the Caprino Romano. Season then serve.

# Cavolo nero and mascarpone cannelloni

SERVES: 4 | PREP TIME: 40 MINUTES | COOKING TIME: 30 MINUTES

## INGREDIENTS

4 tbsp olive oil

2 leeks, finely chopped

2 cloves of garlic, crushed

100 g / 3 ½ oz / 4 cups cavolo nero, stem removed,
finely chopped

250 g / 9 oz / 1 ¼ cups mascarpone

200 g / 7 oz / 1 cup ricotta

1 lemon, zest finely grated

2 tbsp basil, chopped

250 ml / 9 fl. oz / 1 cup tomato passata

12 fresh lasagne sheets

75 g / 2 ½ oz / ¾ cup Pecorino Romano, grated

4 sprigs basil

## METHOD

1. Preheat the oven to 190°C (170°C fan) /
375F / gas 5.

2. Heat 2 tablespoons of the oil in a large
sauté pan and fry the leeks for 8 minutes.
Add the garlic and stir-fry for 2 minutes.

3. Add the cavolo nero to the pan and cover
with a lid. Cook gently for 20 minutes,
stirring halfway through. Tip the mixture
into a bowl and mix with the mascarpone,
ricotta, lemon zest and basil.

4. Spread the passata in an even layer in
a baking dish. Divide the mascarpone
mixture between the lasagne sheets and
roll them up then transfer to the baking dish.

5. Cover the dish with foil and bake
for 30 minutes.

6. Divide the cannelloni between four plates.
Drizzle with the rest of the olive oil,
sprinkle with cheese and garnish with basil.

# Tagliatelle with shimeji and pecorino

SERVES: 4 | PREP TIME: 5 MINUTES | COOKING TIME: 15 MINUTES

## INGREDIENTS

400 g / 14 oz tagliatelle

4 tbsp olive oil

2 cloves of garlic, unpeeled, squashed

1 bay leaf

1 strip lemon zest

225 g / 8 oz / 3 cups shimeji mushrooms, cleaned

50 g / 1 ¾ oz / ¼ cup butter, cubed

75 g / 2 ½ oz / ¾ cup Pecorino Sardo, grated

1 handful basil leaves

## METHOD

1. Boil the pasta in salted water according to the packet instructions or until al dente.

2. Meanwhile, infuse the olive oil with the garlic, bay and lemon in a large sauté pan until it starts to sizzle. Remove with a slotted spoon, then add the mushrooms.

3. Sauté the mushrooms for 8 minutes or until golden brown and any liquid that comes out of them has evaporated. Add the butter to the pan and shake until it melts.

4. Toss the pasta with the mushrooms and divide between four warm bowls.

5. Garnish with Pecorino and basil leaves.

# Gorgonzola ravioli

SERVES: 4 | PREP TIME: 35 MINUTES | COOKING TIME: 5 MINUTES

## INGREDIENTS

500 g / 1 lb 2 oz pasta dough rolled into 2 sheets

### FOR THE FILLING:

10 walnuts

200 g / 7 oz / ¾ cup ricotta

3 tbsp olive oil

250 g / 9 oz Gorgonzola, piccante or dolce

2 ripe pears, cored and quartered

## METHOD

1. Lightly toast the walnuts in a pan. Place in a food processor and mix to a crumble.

2. Stir into the ricotta with 1 tablespoon of oil. Lay a sheet of pasta onto a floured work surface. Place a teaspoon of the mixture at 5 cm (2 in) intervals along the sheet. Brush around each mound with a little beaten egg.

3. Top with the second sheet of pasta. Press down around each mound. Cut out or stamp out with a cutter and lay on a baking tray.

4. Warm the serving plates on a low heat in the oven with chopped Gorgonzola so it starts to melt.

5. Cook the ravioli in boiling water for 2 minutes, remove and drain on kitchen paper. Toss gently with the melted Gorgonzola and top with the pears

# Linguine with mozzarella

SERVES: 4 | PREP TIME: 5 MINUTES | COOKING TIME: 12 MINUTES

## INGREDIENTS

500 g / 1 lb 2 oz / 2 cups linguine

4 tomatoes, chopped

2 tbsp olive oil

2 tbsp basil, chopped

2 balls mozzarella

## METHOD

1.  Cook the pasta according to the packet instructions.

2.  Meanwhile macerate the tomatoes with oil and salt and pepper and leave for 10 minutes.

3.  Once the pasta is drained, return to the pan with the tomatoes, chopped mozzarella and torn basil.

4.  Toss and serve immediately.

# Stuffed conchiglioni with Brie cream

SERVES: 4 | PREP TIME: 5 MINUTES | COOKING TIME: 30 MINUTES

## INGREDIENTS

2 tbsp olive oil

1 onion, finely chopped

2 cloves of garlic, crushed

100 g / 3 ½ oz / 4 cups Swiss chard leaves, washed

250 g / 9 oz / 1 ¼ cups ricotta

¼ tsp nutmeg, freshly grated

24 conchiglioni pasta shells

150 ml / 5 ½ fl. oz / ⅔ cup double (heavy) cream

150 g / 5 ½ oz / 1 ½ cups Brie, rind removed and diced

2 tbsp Parmesan, finely grated

2 tsp cracked black peppercorns

## METHOD

1. Heat the oil in a large sauté pan and fry the onion for 8 minutes. Add the garlic and stir-fry for 2 minutes.

2. Add the chard to the pan and cover with a lid. Let it wilt in its own steam for 4 minutes, stirring halfway through. Tip the mixture into a sieve and squeeze out any excess liquid.

3. Finely chop the chard mixture, then transfer it to a small saucepan and mix with the ricotta and nutmeg. Heat through gently while you cook the pasta.

4. Cook the pasta in boiling salted water according to the packet instructions. Drain well then fill each pasta shell with some of the ricotta mixture.

5. Heat the cream and Brie together until the Brie melts and the sauce starts to bubble.

6. Divide the pasta shells between four plates and spoon over the Brie cream. Sprinkle with Parmesan and cracked black pepper and serve immediately.

# Spinach and ricotta cannelloni

SERVES: 6 | PREP TIME: 15 MINUTES | COOKING TIME: 50 MINUTES

## INGREDIENTS

2 tbsp olive oil

400 g / 14 oz spinach, washed

1 lemon, zest and juice

250 g / 9 oz ricotta

1 egg, beaten

25 g / 1 oz / ¼ cup Parmesan cheese, grated

salt and freshly ground black pepper

150 g / 5 ¼ oz cannelloni

500 g / 1 lb 1 oz passata

a small bunch of fresh basil, chopped

## METHOD

1. Preheat the oven to 180°C (160°C fan) / 350F / gas 4.

2. Heat the olive oil in a pan and add the spinach. Cover and leave to wilt for 5 minutes. Remove from the pan and squeeze out as much moisture from the spinach as possible, then roughly chop it.

3. Combine the spinach, lemon, ricotta, egg and Parmesan in a bowl and beat together. Season.

4. Spoon the ricotta mixture into a piping bag and pipe into the cannelloni. Place the filled pasta in an ovenproof dish.

5. Mix the passata with the basil. Pour over the cannelloni. Cover with foil. Bake in the oven for 45 minutes until the pasta is soft.

# Toasted linguine risotto

SERVES: 2 | PREP TIME: 10 MINUTES | COOKING TIME: 15 MINUTES

## INGREDIENTS

2 tbsp olive oil

200 g / 7 oz linguine, broken into pieces

2 cloves of garlic, minced

400 ml / 13 ½ fl. oz / 1 ⅔ cups chicken stock

50 g Parmesan cheese, grated

sea salt and cracked black pepper

## METHOD

1. Heat the oil in a large pan with a lid over a medium heat.

2. Add the linguine and stir through the oil for 3-5 minutes until toasted and starting to brown.

3. Mix the garlic through the pasta for 1 minute until fragrant.

4. Add a third of the stock and mix though, cover and leave for a couple of minutes until the stock has been absorbed. Repeat until all the stock has been used and the pasta is cooked.

5. Stir through half the cheese and season with salt and black pepper.

6. Serve in warmed bowls and top with the remaining cheese.

# Spinach and ricotta ravioli

SERVES: 2-4 | PREP TIME: 40 MINUTES | COOKING TIME: 10 MINUTES

## INGREDIENTS

300 g / 10 ½ oz / 2 cups pasta grade flour

a pinch of salt

4 large eggs

400 g / 14 oz spinach, washed

1 lemon, zest and juice

250 g / 9 oz ricotta

25 g Parmesan, grated

200 g / 7 oz passata

basil leaves, to garnish

## METHOD

1. Add the flour and salt to a large mixing bowl. Make a well in the centre and add 3 eggs. Incorporate the flour into the eggs using a fork until a dough forms. It should be sticky but not wet. Add more flour if wet, or water if too dry.

2. Turn out onto a floured surface and knead for 10 minutes until you have a smooth dough. Roll into a ball and wrap in cling film before refrigerating for 20 minutes.

3. Using a pasta machine, roll out the dough into two long sheets around 2mm in thickness.

4. Combine the spinach, lemon, ricotta, remaining egg and Parmesan in a bowl and beat together.

5. Spoon the ricotta mixture onto the centre of one pasta sheet at regular intervals, leaving 1 inch between each spoonful. Brush the pasta with water around the filling and place another sheet on top. Press down with your fingers around the filling to expel any air and cut around with a pasta cutter or knife to make your ravioli. Cover and set aside until needed.

6. Bring a large pan of water to the boil. Cook the ravioli for 2-3 minutes until the filling is firm and the pasta cooked.

7. At the same time heat up the passata in a saucepan until warm, season with salt and pepper to taste.

8. Add the cooked ravioli to serving plates and spoon over a little of the warmed passata and garnish with basil leaves.

# Three-cheese agnolotti

SERVES: 2 | PREP TIME: 30 MINUTES | COOKING TIME: 10 MINUTES

## INGREDIENTS

300 g / 10 ½ oz / 2 cups pasta grade flour

a pinch of salt

4 large eggs

100 g / 3 ½ oz / 1 cup Parmesan cheese, grated

200 g / 7 oz ricotta cheese

100 g / 3 ½ oz Dolcelatte, crumbled

truffle oil, to drizzle

## METHOD

1. Add the flour and salt to a large mixing bowl. Make a well in the centre and add three of the eggs. Gradually incorporate the flour into the eggs using a fork until a dough forms. It should be slightly sticky but not too wet, add more flour if needed.

2. Turn out onto a floured surface and knead for 10 minutes until you have a smooth and elastic dough. Roll into a ball and wrap in cling film before refrigerating for 20 minutes.

3. Mix together the three cheeses in a bowl and set aside.

4. Using a pasta machine, roll out the dough into two long sheets around 2 mm in thickness.

5. Using a large round cutter, cut circles the width of the pasta sheet from the long sheets.

6. Place a spoonful of the cheese mixture in the centre of each circle. Beat the remaining egg and brush around the edges of each circle before folding over into a half circle or crescent. Press down gently removing any air from the pocket as you do. Cover and set aside.

7. Boil some salted water in a large saucepan. Once boiling, add the agnolotti to the pan and cook for 2-3 minutes until tender, remove from the pan with a slotted spoon and place onto kitchen paper to drain.

8. Serve on warmed plates with a drizzle of truffle oil.

# Baked pasta in cheese sauce

SERVES: 4-6  |  PREP TIME: 15 MINUTES  |  COOKING TIME: 45 MINUTES

## INGREDIENTS

400 g / 14 oz fusilli pasta

50 g / 1 ¾ oz / ¼ cup unsalted butter

2 cloves of garlic, minced

2 tbsp plain (all-purpose) flour

300 ml / 10 fl. oz / 1 ¼ cups milk

200 g / 7 oz / 2 cups mozzarella, grated

250 g / 9 oz tomatoes, chopped

a handful of fresh parsley, chopped

200 g / 7 oz buffalo mozzarella, sliced

## METHOD

1. Preheat the oven to 180°C (160°C fan) / 350F / gas 4.

2. Cook the pasta in a pan of salted boiling water as per the packet instructions, drain and set aside.

3. Melt the butter in a saucepan over a medium heat. Once frothy add the garlic to the pan and cook for 2-3 minutes until fragrant.

4. Add the flour to the pan and mix through the butter whilst on the heat for a couple of minutes.

5. Remove from the heat and gradually mix in the milk, whisk continuously as you do to prevent any lumps forming. Return to the heat and continue to mix until the sauce thickens.

6. Once thickened add the grated mozzarella and mix through the sauce.

7. Place the pasta into an ovenproof dish and mix through the cheese sauce, tomatoes and chopped parsley. Top with the sliced buffalo mozzarella and bake in the oven for 30 minutes until the cheese has melted and started to turn golden.

# Penne with courgette and mint

SERVES: 4 | PREP TIME: 2 MINUTES | COOKING TIME: 12 MINUTES

## INGREDIENTS

400 g / 14 oz / 4 cups penne

100 ml / 3 ½ fl. oz / ½ cup olive oil

2 cloves of garlic, unpeeled and squashed

3 small courgettes (zucchini), thickly sliced

2 tbsp mint leaves, chopped,
plus a few sprigs to garnish

75 g / 2 ½ oz / ¾ cup Parmesan, finely grated

## METHOD

1.  Boil the pasta in salted water according to
    the packet instructions or until al dente.

2.  Meanwhile, heat the oil in a large sauté pan
    with the garlic until it starts to sizzle, then
    discard the garlic.

3.  Fry the courgettes for 4 minutes on each side
    or until golden brown, then stir in the mint
    and season with salt and pepper.

4.  Drain the pasta and toss with the courgettes,
    then divide between four warm bowls.
    Scatter over the Parmesan and garnish with
    mint sprigs.

# Three-cheese ravioli

SERVES: 2 | PREP TIME: 5 MINUTES | COOKING TIME: 7 MINUTES

## INGREDIENTS

500 g / 1 lb / 2 cups ready-made fresh ravioli, such as spinach and ricotta or wild mushroom

250 g / 9 oz / 1 cup mascarpone

75 g / 3 oz / ⅓ cup Gorgonzola

50 g / 2 oz / ⅓ cup Parmesan, grated

1 clove garlic, peeled

2 sprigs thyme

## METHOD

1. Cook the pasta in boiling salted water according to the packet instructions.

2. Drain, reserving a little of the cooking water and toss with a little oil.

3. Meanwhile heat the mascarpone in a pan with the other cheeses crumbled in.

4. Add the whole garlic clove and thyme, season carefully and stir until the cheeses melt.

5. Fish out the garlic and thyme sprigs.

6. Toss the pasta in the sauce and serve.

# INDEX